DENMARK

BY
MARTIN SYMINGTON

Produced by
Thomas Cook Publishing

Written by Martin Symington
Updated by Robin Gauldie
Original photography by Jesper Westley Jorgensen
Original design by Laburnum Technologies Pvt Ltd

Editing and page layout by Cambridge
Publishing Management Ltd, Unit 2,
Burr Elm Court, Caldecote CB3 7NU
Series Editor: Karen Beaulah

Published by Thomas Cook Publishing
A division of Thomas Cook Tour Operations Ltd
Company Registration No. 1450464 England

PO Box 227, The Thomas Cook Business Park,
Unit 18, Coningsby Road, Peterborough PE3 8SB,
United Kingdom
E-mail: books@thomascook.com
www.thomascookpublishing.com
Tel: +44 (0)1733 416477

ISBN-13: 978-1-84157-692-3

Project Editor: Linda Bass
Production/DTP Editor: Steven Collins

Printed and bound in Italy by: Printer Trento

Cover design by: Liz Lyons Design, Oxford.
Front cover credits: Left © Martin Llado/Lonely Planet; centre © Foto World/Getty Images;
right © Ellen Rooney/Getty Images
Back cover credits: Left © Royalty-Free/Corbis; right © Giovanni Simeone/4 Corners

C o n t e n t s

```
                KEY TO MAPS

   ✈    Airport

   [i]   Information

  147m
   ▲    Mountain

  A201
  E45   Road number

   ☆    Start of walk/tour

   ☀    Viewpoint
```

Traditional costumes are often seen at festivals

Introduction

Denmark may be part of Scandinavia, but this idyllic oasis to the north of Germany has a character entirely its own. Gently rolling hills, majestic beech forests and a coast lined with broad sandy beaches endow this land of several hundred islands and one peninsula with a subtle beauty. Denmark boasts the oldest monarchy and the oldest national flag in the world – both a source of great pride to the Danes, who have ensured that this is one of the most prosperous and egalitarian nations on earth.

Denmark also has a fascinating history that stretches back to the Vikings and beyond. At one time the Danes ruled Scandinavia, northern Germany and large parts of England, and they controlled the Baltic Sea before a succession of ambitious kings brought Denmark to the brink of bankruptcy and defeat in the 17th century. Since then, although much diminished in size and power, the country has been reborn with a renewed artistic and cultural vigour that endures to this day.

Modern Denmark is a small country of a little over 5.3 million people, with

most of its territory accounted for by the Jutland peninsula, pointing finger-like, up from continental Europe towards her Scandinavian partners, Norway and Sweden. Though 90 of its islands are inhabited, the country's main focus is eastwards to Zealand, the island on which stands its capital, Copenhagen, widely recognised as one of northern Europe's great cultural cities.

In many ways Denmark bridges the gap between the Nordic nations and the rest of Europe. The histories of Denmark and Sweden, its immediate neighbour to the north, are inextricably linked (indeed, until the 17th century, southern Sweden was a Danish territory). Their shared tradition is manifest in some liberal and social attitudes – even their languages are related.

Most Danes feel a strong fellowship with their World War II and Cold War allies – Britain and America. Many Danes emigrated to the US in the 19th century, and the world's largest US Independence Day (4 July) celebrations outside the US take place in Aalborg.

Denmark

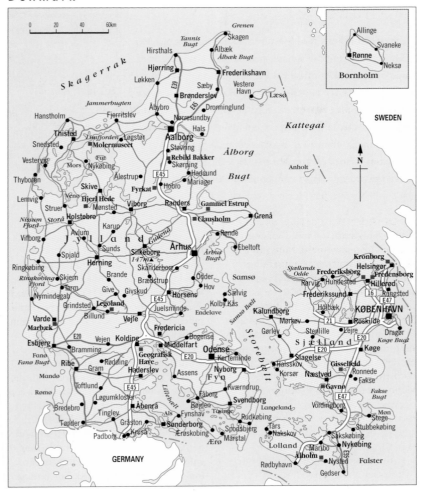

Danes were always great storytellers, and fairytales are a particular speciality. Amid the gentle Danish landscape you will find countless treasures: ancient monuments and the remains of ancient civilisations; glorious castles and fine manor houses; fishing villages of half-timbered cottages; and, of course, the dark impenetrable forests – all of which inspired the fairy stories of the most famous Dane of all, Hans Christian Andersen. Happily, all of this and more still awaits visitors to Denmark in the 21st century.

The land

Denmark covers an area of just over 43,000sq km (16,600sq miles), comprising the Jutland peninsula, a wide arrow of land pointing northwards from Germany, the country's only land frontier, plus 406 islands strewn across the western Baltic. About 90 of these are inhabited, including Zealand (Sjælland), the largest, with Copenhagen (København) on its eastern shore. Of its over 5 million population, 1.5 million Danes are centred in Greater Copenhagen; the rest of the country is sparsely populated. Visit Denmark and you'll pretty much have it all to yourself.

Beach fringing the Kattegat sea

With 7,500km (4,660 miles) of coastline, and nowhere far from the sea, it is hardly surprising that Denmark has always been a seafaring nation. From Viking times through to the 18th century, when Vitus Bering discovered the straits that bear his name between Russia and Alaska, the Danes have been explorers. Fishing and fish processing are among the country's leading industries, supported by maritime trade with most of the world. Summer holidays, weekends and leisure time are spent sailing, or relaxing on great swathes of sandy beach.

In the 20th century, the need for improved communication links both within Denmark and to Sweden provided the impetus for impressive engineering feats of skill. The Storebælts bridge from Funen to Zealand, which opened in 1998, and the Øresund Fixed Link from Copenhagen to southern Sweden which opened in 2000 (*see pp66–7*) have caught the imagination and earned the admiration of the world.

Inland, the terrain on the Danish mainland and the islands alike is smooth, green, fecund and undramatic. The highest point (**Møllehøj**), in central Jutland, is just 171m (561ft) above sea level; the highest waterfall a mere 18m (59ft); and there are no great rivers. But, though lacking extremes, few areas of Denmark are flat. The receding glaciers of the Ice Age left behind numerous folds of gently rolling hills.

West Jutland, facing the North Sea, has the wildest stretch of coast, marked by 300km (186 miles) of beach and wind-ribbed sand dunes, sprinkled with marram grass. The east coast is indented with inlets and fjords, and has a more typically Scandinavian feel. The central parts of the peninsula are characterised by moorland, lakes and undulating countryside. Only on islands such as Lolland and Falster, and on parts of the southern mainland, do you find big open skies and wind-harassed flatlands dotted with windmills for generating electricity.

Agriculture and industry

Long ago forests blanketed most of Denmark, but today only small pockets of conifer and beech wood survive; cultivation claims most of the countryside. About 3 per cent of Denmark's population are farmers or agricultural workers, with the countryside largely given over to cereals, beet and other arable crops, or grazing pasture for dairy herds. Pig farming, which produces the celebrated Danish bacon, is less obviously apparent to the visitor: though intensive, most of it takes place indoors.

Industry, however, has supplanted agriculture as the mainstay of Denmark's economy in recent decades. Nevertheless, compared with other developed industrial countries in Europe, its environmental impact is unobtrusive. Many small towns hide their low-rise factories and light industrial units on discreet estates and shield them from view by trees so that their intrusion on the rural landscape is minimal.

Denmark has only one major city – Copenhagen – home to just over 1.5 million people, almost a third of the population. The next three largest – Århus on Jutland's east coast, Odense on Funen and Aalborg in the north of Jutland – muster not much more than half a million between them.

Lying on a latitude roughly corresponding to Scotland and southern Alaska, Denmark enjoys daylight varying from 17 hours a day in midsummer to 7 hours in midwinter. As with the topography, the climate is generally mild and lacking in extremes. However, standing defiantly outside all these generalisations are the autonomous regions of Greenland and the Faroe Islands (*see pp130–33*).

A Limfjord sunset

History

Around 14,000 years ago	The earliest hunters arrive in the wake of the Ice Age.	**1042**	Death of Hardeknud (Hardicanute), the last Danish king of England.
Around 4000–1800 BC	The Stone Age. Settlers bury their dead within dolmens.	**11th and 12th centuries**	The Church grows as a political force, in close relationship with the Crown.
Around 1800–500 BC	The Bronze Age. Trade with other parts of northern Europe.	**1086**	Knud II (Saint Canute) is murdered by peasants.
Around 500 BC–AD 800	The Iron Age. Grauballe Man and Tollund Man interred in peat bogs near Århus and Silkeborg.	**1157–82**	King Valdemar II subjugates Norway and much of the Baltic coast.
From around AD 500	The Danes, a warrior tribe from Sweden, begin to settle in Jutland.	**1397**	Denmark is united with Norway and Sweden under Queen Margrethe I, daughter of Valdemar II.
Late 8th to mid-11th centuries	The Viking era, with raids on coastal regions of England, Ireland, France, Iceland and Greenland, Russia, Turkey, North Africa and America.	**1523**	Sweden withdraws from the Union.
		1536	The Reformation. Lutheranism established throughout Denmark.
960	King Harald Bluetooth (Harald Blåtand) is baptised. Christianity takes a firm hold in Denmark.	**1563–70**	The inconclusive Seven Years War with Sweden.
		1596–1648	Denmark's 'Golden Age' under the reign of Christian IV.
1016	The Danish King Knud (Canute) becomes King of England. Vikings control much of Britain, Scandinavia and the North Sea.	**1625–57**	Thirty Years War with Sweden. Denmark defeated. The Swedes occupy Jutland and Funen. Treaty of Roskilde.

1660	King Frederick III establishes absolute monarchy.
1801–7	Nelson destroys Danish fleet and occupies Zealand. Denmark sides with Napoleon.
1814	Denmark loses Norway.
1848	Constitutional monarchy under King Frederik VII.
1864	War with Prussia; loss of Schleswig-Holstein.
1914–1918	Denmark remains neutral in World War I.
1920	Parts of Schleswig returned to Denmark under Treaty of Versailles.
1940	Nazis occupy Denmark.
1943	The Danish Resistance Movement is born.
1945	Bornholm bombarded by Soviets after the Germans refuse to surrender.
1947–9	Denmark joins NATO.
1972	Margrethe II succeeds Frederik IX.
1973	Denmark joins the EEC.
1979	Home Rule established in Greenland and the Faroe Islands, which remain within the Kingdom of Denmark, but outside the European Union.
1992–3	Danes first reject then ratify the Maastricht Treaty on European Union in a referendum.
1998	Denmark ratifies the Amsterdam Treaty. A bridge link to Fyn and Zealand is opened.
2000	Denmark votes 'No' to the euro. The Øresund Fixed Link from Zealand to southern Sweden opens.
2001	Danes vote for a new centre-right government headed by Anders Fogh Rasmussen.
2002	Copenhagen's new Metro opens.
2005	Insensitive caricature of Prophet Mohammed in Danish newspaper provokes anti-Danish riots in Muslim countries.
2006	New Curlsberg Gallery reopens after renovation.

Bearded, barbarian warriors, wearing horned helmets and singing bloodthirsty battle-chants at the oars of their dragon-headed longships – or bold pioneers?

The Vikings of Scandinavia have had a bad press ever since their longships first sailed from the fjords of Denmark and Norway to harry the coasts of Britain and Ireland in the 8th century AD.

They were driven to new lands by population pressure – even prosperous Denmark could not support so many people.

Among their first victims were the wealthy, isolated and defenceless monasteries of northeast England. In an era when only clerics could read and write – and when the Church controlled the communications of Europe – they quickly earned an evil reputation.

Yet these pagan warriors were no more brutal and rapacious than the Christians they battled, and Danish Vikings played a huge part in shaping European civilisation. Settling in England, France and Ireland, Danes founded major settlements including Paris, York and Dublin.

Traders as well as looters, Danish ships ranged as far as North Africa and the Mediterranean while their Swedish cousins created a Viking trade route along the Russian rivers to the Black Sea and Byzantium. They had a unique knack of assimilating the cultures of the lands where they settled, and their chiefs intermarried with the daughters of local rulers to create long-lasting dynasties. The famous King Canute (Cnut) of England – who famously failed to turn the rising North Sea tide by sheer willpower – was in fact one of a string of Danish monarchs who claimed the throne of England as well as Denmark.

In England, their heartland was what is now Yorkshire, around their city of Jorvik. The extent of their realm is easily traced by the many place names ending in the Danish '-by' suffix – such as Grimsby, Appleby and many more. On the west coast, they settled in Cumbria, and there was still a Viking settlement in Eskdale in the 11th century.

In France, Danes founded the Duchy of Normandy and in 1066 their French-speaking descendants conquered England – while other Normans fared into the Mediterranean to build sophisticated kingdoms that even challenged the great Byzantine and Holy Roman Empires. The Norman kingdom of Sicily became a beacon of civilised, multicultural tolerance amid the savagery of medieval Europe.

Christendom considered them barbarians, but the Norsemen had a strong sense of justice, and their sophisticated legal code provided the first framework for English and Scots law.

As for the beards and horned helmets, that image owes as much to the movies as to history. The Vikings preferred plain, serviceable helmets, and although archaeologists have found well-preserved longships with elaborate, dragon-like figureheads, such ships were specially built as funeral vessels for Viking lords, not as warships.

Myths and legends have embellished the stories of 9th-century adventurism by Vikings (above); their vessels were similar to these replicas in Roskilde (left)

Governance

Denmark is a constitutional monarchy whose sovereign, Queen Margrethe II, has reigned since 1972. Until 1953 the Danish Constitution specified that only males could ascend the throne. The constitutional change passed by the Folketing, which allowed for a sovereign queen if there were no male heirs, was ratified by referendum. The heir to the throne is Crown Prince Frederik.

The oldest national flag in the world

Parliament
Political power is vested in the Folketing, a 179-seat parliament elected by universal adult suffrage, whose seat is in the Christiansborg Palace in Copenhagen. The voting age is 18. Members of parliament are elected on the 'first-past-the-post' system to represent the country's 135 electoral constituencies. Forty additional seats are reserved for distribution among the parties to redress the imbalance between the number of votes the parties have received nationwide, and the number of seats they have actually won (in order to be represented in the Folketing, a party must gain at least 2 per cent of the total national vote). Two further seats each are reserved for directly elected representatives from Greenland and the Faroe Islands, the two self-governing regions of Denmark.

Parliamentary terms are for a maximum of four years, although it is rare for a full term to be served. When it becomes evident that a government no longer commands a majority in the Folketing, or if a prime minister wants to put the government's case on a particular issue to the people, the procedure is to resign and call fresh elections.

Local government
Denmark has two tiers of local government. The country is divided into 14 county authorities, each with an elected county council and council chairman responsible for policies on such matters as roads and hospitals. The country is further divided into 277 municipalities, each with an elected council and mayor responsible for parochial issues.

Participation in politics
The Danes tend to be avid followers of political events, frequently paying close attention to the lengthy debates in the Folketing, that are carried live on television. Over 90 per cent of the electorate – one of the highest figures in the world – normally exercises its vote.

Recent political events
After the general election of November 2001, in the immediate aftermath of the September 11th terrorist attacks in the US, centre and far-right politicians took

advantage of the attacks to stir up resentment towards immigrants, particularly Muslims, and made significant gains based on campaigns that were strongly condemned by international organisations including the United Nations. Denmark's reputation as a modern, liberal, egalitarian society that welcomed immigrants and prided itself on its integration policies was eradicated virtually overnight. The new centre-right government, headed by Anders Fogh Rasmussen (leader of the Liberal Party), with the far-right Danish People's Party as third-place power brokers, wasted no time in tightening immigration laws (to the extent that their validity under human rights agreements was questioned), and slashing overseas aid budgets. As well as this, the government has begun to cut back welfare state provision and funding for the arts in a bid to stop the already high levels of tax increasing further. A North Sea oil bonanza, announced in early 2002, is still helping to swell the government's coffers. It helped them to remain in power with a win in the February 2005 elections.

The Danish parliament sits in the magnificent Christiansborg Palace

Culture

Despite the perception of the rest of the world that 'Scandinavian' is a generic term that encompasses all the people of Denmark, Sweden and Norway, the three races are very different from each other. Danes have more in common with Germans, in fact, and are proud of their relaxed attitudes on subjects like alcohol and smoking (much frowned upon in Sweden). There is, however, one element of Danish culture that is utterly unique: Jante Law.

Amateur painters reflect the relaxed Danish lifestyle

Sooner or later most visitors to Denmark discover that much Danish behaviour is still to some extent governed by **Jante Law**. Jante is a fictional village from a 1933 novel by Danish writer Axel Sandemose. The village is typically Danish in that the overriding social imperative that governs its inhabitants' behaviour is: 'Nobody is anything special. Don't try and stand out or pretend that you are better than anybody else at anything'. Jante Law is a crystallisation of all that Sandemose despised in the Danish mentality – its homogeneity, lack of ambition, repressed envy and lack of vision – and many would say that little has changed. Indeed, Queen Margrethe herself once complained publicly that this attitude still inhibits Danes, to their detriment.

More positively, in theory everybody is equal in Denmark – another Jante Law tenet. This is not an empty ideological notion, but a genuine Danish belief that leads the nation to accept a degree of social conformity that astounds other Europeans. It is, however, conformity of Denmark's own egalitarian devising. Hence the massively high taxes, paid remarkably willingly, the almost nonexistent class distinctions and the easy interchange of traditional roles among the sexes. However, black, Middle Eastern and Asian immigrants might well dispute this claim of equality.

Attitudes

Scaremongering by far-right parties has raised fears of a racist backlash that is very much at odds with the reality of one of Europe's more sensible and tolerant societies, and it is very rare that visitors with varying ethnic backgrounds sense any direct hostility.

One curious contradiction of modern Danish society is that everybody is expected to conform in tolerating different lifestyles even where these lifestyles are themselves antisocial or intolerant. The continued existence of the Christiania 'social experiment' (an alternative commune in the centre of Copenhagen) exemplifies the paradox (see p29).

The notorious Danish reputation for sexual promiscuity is a myth that has its origins in the Danes' genuinely liberated attitude to sexual matters (*see p17*). Copenhagen's sex industry is very small-scale and centres around what is one of Europe's least threatening red-light districts.

Copenhagen and many other Danish cities have thriving gay scenes, with very low levels of animosity from the heterosexual community. Gay marriage in Denmark takes the form of a legally binding agreement that gives both parties equal rights.

As far as heterosexual marriage is concerned, the institution remains popular, with around 35,000 couples tying the nuptial knot each year, usually after having first lived together. In over half these cases, couples opt for a church wedding. Divorce, however, is easily obtained and about 17,000 marriages end this way each year. It is perfectly acceptable for couples to live together and bring up a family without marrying. More than 100,000 couples live in so-called 'paperless marriages' with children born of this arrangement or from previous relationships.

A mix of cultures is clearly visible in the heart of the city

Enjoying a bright summer's day...

occasions such as a family member's birthday. The Dannebrog, as the Danish flag is known, is highly cherished by the Danes and is very much part of their everyday life.

Another fundamental element of Danish culture is the notion of *hygge* (*see p19*). Visitors invited inside a Danish home find that creating a feeling of *hygge* is central to all entertaining. Candles invariably flicker, fires burn if it is winter, and the guest is pampered. In summer, cosy gatherings on the terrace or in the garden create a similar sense of intimate sharing in family life. No greater compliment can be paid to a host than to say that you have had a *hygge* time.

The Danish home

Young couples, whether married or living together, generally spend their first few years in a rented apartment. When children arrive, and if they can afford it, many then move to their own house – usually with three or four rooms and a small garden. These are the neat modern houses, built over the last 30 years, that can be seen on the outskirts of every Danish town and city.

Inside, the decor tends to be stylish rather than traditional; as with the rest of the world, modern, Danish-designed furniture remains highly desired. The focus of every living room is often the television set: it has been estimated that Danes spend 40 per cent of their leisure time in front of the small screen.

A flagpole stands in the garden of about 1 million homes, from which the red and white 'Dannebrog' flutters on national holidays, or on private

Religious observance

Religious observance in Denmark is low, with about 4 per cent of the population regularly attending church. Sunday services in the hundreds of beautiful churches around the country are usually attended by just a scattering of older folk, mainly women. Only at Christmas do the pews fill up.

Even so, the National Church of Denmark, which is Evangelical Lutheran, does command a genuine respect, with about 87 per cent of the population being at least nominal members. Despite their non-belief, it remains important for many people to be baptised, confirmed, married and buried according to church rites. More surprisingly, a special tax, the equivalent of 0.8 per cent of salary, is levied in Denmark on behalf of the church, and though the tax is voluntary, amazingly, 85 per cent of people pay up.

Sexual equality

Denmark's reputation for sexual equality is, in many ways, justified. Danes are a courteous people and tend to be civil and thoughtful in their everyday dealings with each other.

Denmark was an early pioneer of the rights of women and children. Sexual harassment in public or in the workplace tends to be less of a problem than in many other parts of the world. An egalitarian attitude between the sexes prevails, with men expected to take a greater share in household and family responsibilities than in many European countries. The gap in wages and salaries between men and women is also significantly smaller than in most of Europe, and gender discrimination is prohibited.

Child-minding and domestic chores are often shared by partners, but many women complain that their men lack enthusiasm when it comes to putting their egalitarian beliefs into practice. The law guarantees generous maternity and paternity leave, after which time both partners expect to return to work. Most couples hand the bulk of their child-minding over to public day-care centres, nurseries and kindergartens. Options such as one parent remaining at home to look after the children, or of employing a private nanny, are not only economically unfeasible to most Danes, they also break Jante Law (*see p14*).

...and a game in King's Garden at Rosenborg Castle

Impressions

Denmark is one of the easiest countries in the world to travel around in. There is a fast and highly efficient air, rail and road network that makes virtually any part of this close-knit country accessible from anywhere else in half a day. Public transport, which generally has helpful English-speaking staff, is punctual, clean, safe and easy to use.

The picturesque streets are pedestrian friendly

Getting around

Information on nationwide transport is available from tourist offices and websites such as *www.DSB.dk* (for trains) and *www.HT.dk* (for buses and other forms of transport). These should always be the first port of call in any city or town because of the excellent local information they provide.

Roads are very much secondary in the Danish scheme of things, though they are generally adequate for the country's 1.6 million cars and serious traffic jams are rare.

In Denmark the cyclist is king. Everyone in Denmark cycles, regardless of age or class, and there are excellent cycle lanes in all towns, cities and most of the countryside. Cyclists usually have right of way in traffic and, particularly in Copenhagen, they take no prisoners. You'll need nerves of steel to dice in the cycle lanes during rush hour!

In Copenhagen and many other places it is easy for visitors to do as the Danes do and use two-wheel transport. In the capital, a fleet of colourful pay-as-you-go bikes is available from

No, you aren't seeing things! Note the Copenhagen sticker...

Cyclists are as at home on Copenhagen streets as on wilder tracks

some 20 locations around the city – just put 20 kroner in the slot and away you go. There are bike rental agencies at most resorts, and in Copenhagen and Aarhus there are even rickshaw-style pedal taxis.

Hygge

Hygge is an often-used, uniquely Danish and untranslatable term. It is most often described as a kind of cosiness or homeliness to be found at the heart of Danish life. The obvious symbols of *hygge* are the candles that burn at the table at every meal, including breakfast – the per-capita consumption of wax in

Denmark must be the highest on the planet! In practice, *hygge* translates into the warmth of sitting round a fire with a blanket and a hot drink, chatting (not discussing or arguing) or watching television on evenings and weekends with family and friends, when Swedes or Norwegians would more typically be out skiing or hiking in the forest.

In the summer, cyclists are likely to find wooden trolleys left by the roadside laden with thermos flasks of iced tea, jars of honey, speckled brown eggs and other homely goodies; they are left unattended, with honesty boxes to pay for whatever takes your fancy. That's *hygge* too.

Danes gather on a leafy thoroughfare for a casual chat

Language

Other Scandinavians describe the Danish language as a disease of the throat. Those who try to learn it must train their vocal cords to produce rasping consonants of a kind excluded from polite conversation in most cultures, and to swallow the middle of every word. Happily for the English-speaker, nobody in Denmark expects anybody else to speak their language. English is almost universally spoken, with an extraordinary degree of fluency, making communication rarely a problem. The relationship between the English and the Danish takes the form of a sort of linguistic valve; Danes flow effortlessly into English, but the reverse is nigh on impossible. That said, the odd *tusind tak* (a thousand thanks) will be much appreciated.

Etiquette

The Danes like to think of themselves as a casual people. Dress tends to be comfortable and functional, rather than formal or showy, even in the best restaurants or at the opera. Nudity is the norm on many beaches and nobody bats an eyelid; in summer when the sun shines, women feel free to sunbathe topless in city parks and other public places.

Conversely, visitors from countries where kisses and embraces are the norm sometimes find Danes socially cold, and rather formal. At parties, for example, new arrivals are expected to tour the crowd shaking hands and introducing themselves, and woe betide anyone who arrives late. If a Dane says dinner is at 7pm, the plates will be sitting on the table by 7.15pm.

Lifestyle

On the whole, Danes tend to be well travelled, and young people think nothing of setting off on extended back-packing journeys round the world. Five weeks' annual paid holiday is the established norm in the Danish labour market, with those who can afford it taking long-haul holidays; thousands more regularly head off for cheap beach holidays in the Mediterranean or the Canary Islands.

But as you might also expect from such an inward-looking folk, the majority of Danes still prefer to holiday at home, mainly in summer cottages which people either own or rent, almost always by the sea. These are also frequently used at weekends, from spring through to the autumn.

Wide-open squares without the usual bustle of tourists are part of Denmark's charm

Copenhagen city plan (*see pp40–41 for walk route*)

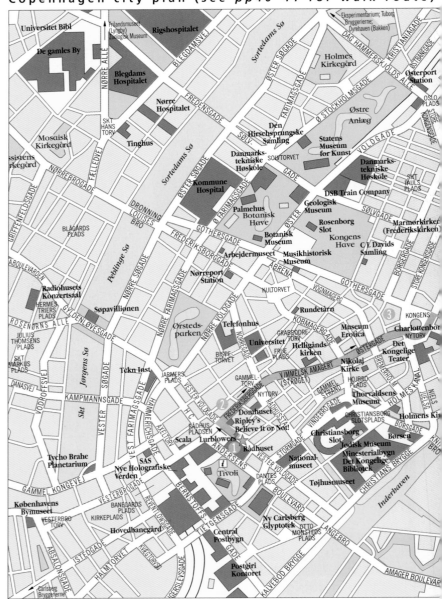

Copenhagen

København

Copenhagen is the most vibrant capital city in Scandinavia. As the focus of Danish political, commercial and cultural life, it is, in every sense, the national capital. For many visitors – both tourists and business travellers alike – Copenhagen *is* Denmark, and you'd certainly hear no argument about that from the locals.

Other than in the capital, Denmark is characterised by calm, understated provincialism. Some say that the vitality of the nation is sapped by Copenhagen's dominance, and that the contrast between the capital and the rest of the country is absolute. Yet many national traits, comparable to those found elsewhere in the country, are clearly evident in Copenhagen.

The population of Greater Copenhagen is a little over 1.5 million, of whom only half a million live in central Copenhagen. The city is uncommonly user-friendly, with many of its attractions within easy walking distance. Exploring on foot is itself a pleasure, and there are many pedestrianised streets. High-rise buildings are few and far between and the city is characterised by green expanses and waterscapes. There is relatively little motor traffic; great store is set by pedal power as a means of urban transport, with ample tracks provided especially for cyclists.

Denmark's imperial face shows itself at the daily changing of the Royal Guard

Then and now

In the 12th century, King Valdemar I the Great gave a small fishing village, then known simply as Havn (Harbour) to the powerful Bishop Absalon. To defend it, the bishop built a fortress on the island now known as Slotsholmen. The town grew into a key commercial port, becoming known as Københmands Havn (Merchants' Harbour), hence its present name. In 1443 it became the Danish capital, expanding hugely in the late 16th and early 17th century during the reign of Christian IV, whose grand monuments are so much a part of the modern city.

Today's Copenhagen is strewn with castles, churches and other historic monuments. It also has an extraordinary wealth of museums, making it one of the richest cities anywhere for the sightseer. All this is enlivened, particularly in summer, by a vibrant street life, with outdoor cafés, restaurants and entertainers everywhere, especially along Strøget. Stretching between Rådhuspladsen and Kongens Nytorv, this is said to be the longest pedestrian precinct in Europe. By night, Copenhagen pulses in its bars, pubs and live-music clubs.

Amalienborg Plads (Amalienborg Square)

King Frederik V has pride of place at the centre of this octagonal cobbled piazza. He takes the form of a neoclassical equestrian statue, overlooked by the four rococo palaces that house different members of the Danish royal family.

When the Queen is at home (a flag flies to signify this), there is a daily changing of the guard ceremony. Soldiers wearing blue trousers, red tunics and huge bearskin hats keep imperial nostalgia alive, marching to the strains of a military band. The parade leaves Rosenborg castle at 11.30am daily to arrive at Amalienborg at noon.

The Amalienborg Museum, housed in Levetzau Palace, one of the four palaces around the square, contains several rooms filled with royal memorabilia plus recreations of private rooms of past monarchs.

By the Amaliehaven docks, just north of Nyhavn. Museum entrance from Levetzau Palace, Amalienborg Plads. Tel: 33 12 21 86; www.amalienborgmuseet.dk. Open: daily, May–Oct 10am–4pm; Nov–Apr 11am–4pm. Admission charge.

The Black Diamond

When it opened in 1999, the new extension to the Royal Library took Denmark by storm. This stunning granite and glass building is now one of the city's most memorable landmarks. It houses not just the country's pre-eminent collection of 200,000 books and manuscripts, but a concert house, exhibition space, book shop, restaurant and café.

Entrance Søren Kierkegaards Plads 1. Tel: 33 47 47 47; www.kb.dk. Main building open: Mon–Sat 10am–7pm. Closed: Sun. Admission charge to exhibitions.

Botanisk Have (Botanical Gardens)

Wander among more than 15,500 labelled trees, shrubs and herbs in 10ha (25 acres) of landscaped gardens, originally laid out between 1871 and 1874. For tropical and subtropical plants there is a large domed Victorian-style greenhouse, inspired by London's Kew Gardens. Also under glass are collections of cacti, begonias, orchids and carnivorous plants.

Entrances at Gothersgade 128 and Øster Farimagsgade 2B. Tel: 35 32 22 22; www.botanic-garden.ku.dk. Gardens open: daily, Oct–Apr 8.30am–4pm except Mon; May–Sept 8.30am–6pm. Palm House open: daily 10am–3pm. Cactus House open: Wed, Sat & Sun 1–2pm. Free admission.

Copenhagen tourist information, *Vesterbrogade 4A. Tel: +45 70 22 24 42; www.visitcopenhagen.com*

Botanists from around the world seek out treasures at Botanisk Have

When a 31-year-old woman of intelligence and talent ascended the Danish throne in 1972, a palpable gust of fresh air swept through the world's oldest monarchy. Queen Margrethe II was the nation's first female monarch for nearly 600 years. With her ascension, the stuffiness characteristic of the reign of her father, Frederik IX, simply evaporated. In an indirect sense, Margrethe was also elected democratically; the constitutional revision allowing female succession, when there were no male heirs, was approved by referendum in 1953.

As Queen, Margrethe involves herself directly in national affairs. Her constitutional duties as head of state involve foreign tours, regular meetings with government and diplomatic functions. She has made the most impact on Danish life, however, on issues of her own choosing. In her traditional New Year address, and in frequent media interviews, she encourages her subjects to give generously to Third World charities and to take care of their own elderly.

She has gently chided the nation for overdoing the 'Jante' mentality that scorns anyone who tries to stand out, suggesting that this contributes to a collective loss of self-confidence. Most Danes listen to her with great respect. They are also proud of her many personal achievements which go beyond her monarchical duties.

She has translated Simone de Beauvoir's novel *Tous les Hommes sont Mortelles* (*All Men are Mortal*) from French into Danish, and she designed the set for a television production of Hans Christian Andersen's story, *The Shepherdess and the Chimneysweep*. She also devotes a great deal of time to her family, including her aged mother,

Queen Ingrid, her husband and consort, Prince Henrik, and her two sons, Crown Prince Frederik and Prince Joachim. Her image, however, is not one of a 'bicycling monarch'. Royal trappings, such as the changing of the guard, are maintained. She usually travels in a luxury limousine.

Few Danes will talk about their queen with anything other than affection (though other members of her family are not so wholeheartedly endorsed). Among the small minority of republican-minded Danes, many would vote for Margrethe as their first president.

Facing page and above: Queen Margrethe at her birthday celebrations
Right: the crown jewels of Denmark

Oarsmen row past the government buildings in the Christiansborg Palace complex

Christiansborg Slot (Christiansborg Palace)

Christiansborg Palace is the cradle of Copenhagen's history and the political nerve centre of the modern state. Its origins lie in the 12th-century castle built by Bishop Absalon on the island of Slotsholmen, paving the way for Copenhagen eventually to become the capital of Denmark. Eight bridges span the canals surrounding the island.

There are still some vestiges of the original castle to explore by descending into the quiet, dank basement to see the **Palace Ruins**. The palace complex today is dominated by a dense cluster of grandiose green-roofed government buildings, including the **Folketing** (the National Parliament), the prime minister's office, the Supreme Court and various royal institutions. Several of these can also be visited as individual attractions. One not to be missed is a tour (in English) of the sumptuous Renaissance **Royal Reception Rooms**, with their chandeliers, gilded ceilings, silk wall-hangings, priceless furniture and paintings. The rooms are still used by the Queen for state occasions and official entertaining.

There is less to detain you in the Folketing, which is open to the public at certain times, even when parliament is in session. The exhibition of state coaches, in the old **Royal Stables**, is also worth a quick visit, as is the atmospheric **Theatre Museum**.

Christiansborg Palace Ruins.
Tel: 33 92 64 92. Open: Oct–Apr,
Tue–Sun 10am–4pm; May–Sept,
daily 10am–4pm.
Admission charge.

Folketing tel: 33 37 55 00;
www.folketing.dk. All other palace
attractions tel: 33 92 65 33; www.slotte.dk.
Open: Oct–June, daily tours every hour
10am–3pm except at noon; July–mid-Aug,
daily tours every hour 10am–3pm except
at noon & on Sat; mid-Aug–Sept, daily
tours at 2pm & 3pm, except on Sat.
Free admission.
Royal Reception Rooms. Tours in English:
May–Sept, daily at 11am, 1pm & 3pm;
Oct–Apr, on Tue, Thur, Sat & Sun at 3pm.
Admission charge.
Royal Stables & Coaches. Open:
May–Sept, Fri–Sun 2–4pm; Oct–Apr,
Sat & Sun 2–4pm. Admission charge.
Theatre Museum. Open: Tue–Thur
11am–3pm, Sat & Sun 1–4pm.
Closed: Mon & Fri. Admission charge.

Christiania

The 'hippie free state' of Christiania, founded in 1971 when New Age squatters took over a disused army barracks in the Christianshavn district, is as controversial as ever. Christiania has been tolerated ever since as a social experiment, subject to its own rules (which include tolerance of the sale and use of cannabis, but not of hard drugs), despite periodic campaigns by conservative factions to close it down – and, since 2001, increased police harassment. There is a scruffy, laid-back ambience to its beaten earth roads, shops, organic cafés and restaurants, and visitors are free to wander around, buy trinkets or eat at the various cafés. Cameras should be left behind – photography is not welcome and is banned on 'Pusher Street', the main thoroughfare where cannabis is openly sold.

Hans Christian Andersen's Adventure World

Opened in April 2004, this museum is Copenhagen's tribute to the most famous Dane of all, with memorabilia, documents and displays surrounding the life of the fairy-tale writer, poet, artist and novelist. Though born in Odense, HC Andersen spent most of his life, when not travelling, in his beloved Copenhagen.
Radhuspladsen 57. Tel: 33 32 31 31;
www.hcandersen.com. Open: daily
10am–7pm. Admission charge.

Riotous graffiti adorns the houses in Christiania

Hirschsprungske Samling (Hirschsprung Collection)

Heinrich Hirschsprung (1836–1908) was a tobacco magnate, art collector and philanthropist who donated his extensive collection of mainly Danish 19th-century paintings and sculptures to the nation. The museum stands in Østre Anlæg park, to the north of the city, looking out across ornamental lakes. The collection includes many examples of the art of the Danish Golden Age, as well as works by the Skagen school (*see p110*) and the Funen painters (*see p71*). *Stockholmsgade 20. Tel: 35 42 03 36;* *www.hirschsprung.dk. Open: Wed–Mon 11am–4pm. Closed: Tue. Admission charge.*

Lille Havfrue (Little Mermaid)

Some visitors are a mite disappointed to discover that Copenhagen's most enduring symbol, a diminutive bronze figure sitting on a rock, is located in isolation in the city's industrial docks. The sculpture is the work of Edvard Eriksen and depicts the title character from Hans Christian Andersen's fairy story *The Little Mermaid*. It was donated to the city of Copenhagen in 1913 by

Hans Christian Andersen's Little Mermaid holding vigil over the harbour at Copenhagen symbolises the country's relationship with the sea

Carl Jacobsen of the Carlsberg Breweries. The mermaid's graceful posture and modest simplicity captured the imagination of sailors. Soon, none left the port without making a pilgrimage to see her – a symbol of innocence to whom they appealed for forgiveness for their misdemeanours while in port. The sailors carried the mermaid's tale around the globe, and few tourists leave Copenhagen without seeing her.

The Little Mermaid is located on a rock by the quayside about 500m (1,640ft) north of the Amalienborg Plads.

Jødisk Museum (Jewish Museum)

Highlighting the hidden history of Copenhagen's Jewish community and the remarkable story of how Danes helped to spirit Jewish refugees to safety in neutral Sweden, this moving museum opened in 2004.

Bibliotekshaven. Tel: 33 11 22 18; www.jewmus.dk. Open: Tue–Fri 1–4pm, Sat–Sun noon–5pm. Closed: Mon. Admission charge.

Marmorkirken (Marble Church)

Known officially as Frederikskirken (Frederik's Church), this is Copenhagen's most arresting place of worship. Its large dome was inspired by those of St Paul's Cathedral, in London, and St Peter's Basilica, in Rome. Frederik V ordered the construction of the church in 1749. He visualised the church becoming the centrepiece of a splendid imperial district to be built around what is now Amalienborg, which he planned to call Frederiksgade.

Lack of funds put paid to the project, and work on the Marmorkirken was

The distinctive Marmorkirken was designed as an imperial showpiece

shelved in 1770. Finally, a rich financier, Carl Frederik Tietgen, paid for its completion in 1894. Today, its imperious exterior is guarded by massive marble columns and statues of great figures from Danish history, all of which give the church a strong sense of being a national monument. Inside, the huge circular nave is adorned with colourful frescoes.

Frederiksgade 4. Tel: 33 15 01 44; www.marmorkirken.dk. Open: Mon–Thur 10am–5pm, Wed until 6pm, Fri–Sun noon–5pm. Free admission.

Minor museums

Copenhagen has scores of museums covering just about every conceivable speciality interest. Among them are museums devoted to amber, pipes and tobacco, to the history of the Danish theatre, of post and telegraphy (not to be confused with the Telephone Museum), of medical history, workers, geology, eroticism and ship building. Think of a subject, however obscure, and there is a fairly good chance that Copenhagen has a museum, tucked away somewhere, that is dedicated to exploring its scope, history and relevance to the modern world.

Most of these minor museums are listed in *Copenhagen This Week*, available free from the tourist office, or on the Copenhagen tourist board website, *www.visitcopenhagen.dk*. There are a number that deserve special mention:

Arbejdermuseet
(Workers' Museum)
Shows how Danish working life and the home life of workers has changed since the 1870s.
Rømersgade 22. Tel: 33 93 25 75; www.arbejdermuseet.dk

Arkitekturcentret
(Architecture Centre)
Regular changing exhibitions on contemporary and historical architectural themes.
Strandgade 27B. Tel: 32 75 19 30; www.dac.dk

Carlsberg Besøgscenter (Carlsberg Visitors Centre Exhibition)
On the famous Danish brewer.
Gamle Carlsberg Vej 11. Tel: 33 27 13 14; www.visitcarlsberg.dk

Tøjhusmuseet
(Royal Arsenal Museum)
This museum has a collection of weaponry and exhibitions charting the rise and fall of Denmark as an imperial power.
Tøjhusgade 3. Tel: 33 11 60 37; www.thm.dk. Closed: Mon.

Medicinhistorisk Museum
(Medical History Museum)
Often gory and gruesome, this is nevertheless a fascinating collection of medical artifacts.
Bredgade 62. Tel: 35 32 38 00; www.mhm.ku.dk

Musikhistorisk Museum
(Musical History Museum)
A superb collection of musical instruments from around the world, spanning the last 1,000 years.
Åbenrå 30. Tel: 33 11 27 26; www.musikhistoriskmuseum.dk. Open: Oct–Apr, Mon, Wed, Sat & Sun 1–3.50pm; May–Sept, Fri–Wed 1–3.50pm. Closed: Thur.

Zoologisk Museum
(Zoological Museum)
First-rate, and includes a diorama of 'The Deer in the Danish Beech Forest' made with 18,000 beech leaves.
Universitetsparken 15. Tel: 35 32 10 01; www.zoologiskmuseum.dk. Closed: Mon.

Oplevelsemuseum
(Ripley's Believe It or Not!)
Great fun for all the family, based on Ripley's *Believe It or Not* stories, with a few surprises. You have been warned!
Rådhuspladsen 57. Tel: 33 91 89 91; www.ripleys.dk

Museum Erotica
See box opposite.

Pornography

Denmark's reputation as a hotbed of sexual freedom and flagrant erotica is long out of date. Today, far from being a voyeur's paradise, Copenhagen is squeaky clean when compared with most European capitals.

For a brief spell in the 1960s, Denmark was perceived as the world's most sexually liberated nation and – thanks to relaxation of laws banning explicit sexual images – as the world capital of pornography.

By then, Denmark had already achieved a degree of gender equality way ahead of most of Europe, and a liberal attitude towards sex and erotica was just one facet of generally enlightened social attitudes.

That was more than 40 years ago. Since then the rest of Europe has caught up with Denmark, and hard-core porn is less flagrantly peddled

MUSEUM EROTICA

Just off Copenhagen's main shopping street, this museum illustrates the history of erotica through the ages, with images that become increasingly explicit as viewers move up the building. On the top floor video screens show hard-core porn, and gay and 'shock' themed rooms add to the titillation.
Kobmagergade 24. Tel: 33 12 03 11;
www.museumerotica.dk.
Open: daily May–Sept 10am–11pm;
Oct–Apr 11am–8pm.
Admission charge.

---

than in most European countries. While cities such as Amsterdam, Hamburg and Brussels have clearly defined red-light districts where pornography and commercial sex are openly on sale, the visitor in search of titillation will find Copenhagen a disappointment.

Even Nyhavn – the formerly rambunctious waterfront that once satisfied the baser urges of sailors returning from long ocean voyages – has just one surviving striptease club, and the famous Museum Erotica is the exception rather than the rule. This is partly due to sensible Danish attitudes. For many Danes, pornography is no longer seen as a liberating force, but as a form of exploitation.

Entrance to the Museum Erotica

National Museet
(National Museum)

Denmark's principal museum of culture and history reopened in 1992 in airy glass-plated glory after extensive renovation and expansion. This included covering the entrance courtyard with a glass roof to create a vast atrium surrounded by balconies.

A chronological tour of the museum starts with the rich collection of Bronze and Iron Age finds. Don't miss the golden, spiral-decorated sun worshippers' disc, mounted on a horse-drawn chariot, unearthed in Zealand and dated to about 1400 BC.

Following on are rows of enigmatic rune stones, rooms full of Viking weaponry and a good section on medieval Danish life, with original peasant tools and handicrafts, plus some religious statues and gilded altarpiece carvings.

But the collection is not limited to Danish finds. The Ethnographic Collection, with pieces from around the world, including Islamic art, oriental collections and an inspiring exhibition on Inuit life in Greenland, is also fascinating. The latter brings the section neatly back to the museum's avowed purpose of offering 'an understanding of Denmark's relationship with the rest of the world over the last 10,000 years'.

Elegant sculpture at the National Museum

The Children's Museum, consisting of a variety of temporary and permanent exhibitions, gives youngsters a glimpse of life in other cultures and other ages with various interactive activities – a Bedouin tent and a reconstructed Viking ship, to be climbed into and played on, seem to be especial favourites.
Ny Vestergade 10. Tel: 33 13 44 11; www.natmus.dk. Open: Tue–Sun 10am–5pm. Closed: Mon. Free admission.

Ny Carlsberg Glyptotek (New Carlsberg Gallery)

In 1888 Carl Jacobsen of the Carlsberg brewing company donated this extensive collection of art to the nation. Jacobsen's particular fascination was with all things classical, as borne out by the rooms filled with ancient Egyptian, Greek, Roman and Etruscan relics. The art collection includes French Impressionist works by, among others, Monet, Pissarro, Degas and Cézanne, now displayed in a stunning modernist extension to the original building, by Danish master builder Henning Larsen. The gallery reopened in 2006 after a complete renovation.
Dantes Plads 7. Tel: 33 41 81 41; www.glyptoteket.dk. Open: Tue–Sun 10am–4pm. Closed: Mon. Free admission on Wed & Sun; admission charge on other days.

Orlogsmuseet (Naval Museum)

This museum tells the story of the Danish Navy through 300 minutely detailed models of ships. There are also several life-sized vessels, including the Royal Barge. Some vessels can be

Rosenborg Castle stands in an expanse of glorious parkland and gardens

boarded, and there is a play ship for children.
Overgaden oven Vandet 58. Tel: 32 54 63 63; www.orlogsmuseet.dk. Open: Tue–Sun noon–4pm. Closed: Mon. Admission charge.

Rosenborg Slot (Rosenborg Castle)

There are three compelling reasons for visiting Rosenborg. First, wandering about the **Rosenborg Have**, also known as the Kongens Have (King's Gardens), surrounding the castle provides a superb introduction to the treasures in store. Spread over almost 12ha (30 acres), Copenhagen's oldest public park is dotted with statues and pavilions. From spring to summer it is ablaze with blooms that mellow into rich autumn colours. Second, the castle itself, built in 1606–34 by Christian IV as a summer palace outside the city walls, is a rare opportunity for an informal, intimate glimpse of Danish royal life over the centuries.

The tour is arranged in chronological order, through rooms stuffed with the riches accumulated by various kings and now part of the Danish Royal Collection. The oldest is Christian IV's Winter Room, hung with scores of Renaissance paintings. His oak-panelled and Chinese-lacquered study and his tiled bathroom have been preserved in their original state. Other highlights include Frederik IV's baroque stuccoed ceiling in the Great Hall, and his bizarre chamber with its mirrored walls and ceiling.

Finally, rounding off a visit to Rosenborg, is **De Danske Kongers Kronologiste Samling** (the Danish crown jewels), a separate museum in the castle basement. Pride of place among the dazzling treasures amassed by Danish royalty over the last 500 years goes to Christian IV's diamond- and pearl-studded gold crown.

Øster Voldgade 4A. Tel: 33 15 32 86. Castle and Crown Jewels Museum open: daily, Jan–Apr 11am–2pm (closed: Mon); May 10am–4pm; June–Aug 10am–5pm; Sept 10am–4pm; Oct 11am–3pm; Nov & Dec 11am–2pm (closed: Mon). Admission charge.

Legions of tulips in the King's Gardens give way to other blooms in summer

Rundetårn (Round Tower)

This sturdy circular tower is one of Copenhagen's most distinctive landmarks, commanding views over the whole city and beyond from the platform at its 35-m (115-ft) summit. It was built in 1642 on the orders of Christian IV, as part of a new university, to house a students' church, a library and, at the top, an astronomical observatory. It still functions as an observatory, one of the oldest in Europe. A spiral walkway, over 200m (650ft) long, was specially constructed around the tower to enable telescopes to be carried to the top.

The original church and library were destroyed by a fire in 1728, although the tower itself survived. Both have been reconstructed. Halfway up, a door leads into the library hall, which is now a venue for regularly changing exhibitions of art, culture, history and science. The baroque church is peaceful, missing out on the huge numbers of tourists who come only to climb the tower. *Købmagergade 52A. Tel: 33 73 03 73; www.rundetaarn.dk. Open: Sept–May, Mon–Sat 10am–5pm, Sun noon–5pm; June–Aug, Mon–Sat 10am–8pm, Sun noon–8pm. Observatory open: mid-Oct–mid-Mar, Tue & Wed 7–10pm; mid-June–mid-Aug, Sun 1–4pm. Closed: mid-Mar–mid-June & mid-Aug–mid-Oct. Admission charge.*

Statens Museum for Kunst (National Gallery)

Denmark's National Gallery has a rich collection of European and Danish paintings and sculpture, ranging from Byzantine icons, through 17th-century European works, to modern art. The galleries, with their stately arches, ceilings and mosaic floors, are a fitting backdrop for the works of Dutch, Flemish and Italian masters, along with French Impressionists and 20th-century artists, including Braque, Matisse and Picasso.

Of particular importance, however, is the extensive Danish collection, with examples of every major artist represented, from the Golden Age to the present. In 1998 a vast and airy new extension opened overlooking the park behind the museum which is now home to the impressive 20th-century collection and the children's museum. *Sølvgade 48–50. Tel: 33 74 84 94; www.smk.dk. Open: Tue & Thur–Sun 10am–5pm; Wed 10am–8pm. Closed: Mon. Admission charge.*

Thorvaldsens Museum

In 1838 the Copenhagen-born sculptor Bertel Thorvaldsen (1770–1844) presented his classical Greek- and Roman-influenced works, plus his life-long collection of paintings and antiques, to his native city. A condition, however, was that a suitable building be found to house them. Consequently, an exquisite neoclassical house, with a mural-decorated façade, was erected to become the Thorvaldsens Museum and mausoleum where the sculptor is buried.

It is well worth passing by simply to see the exterior, though art lovers will be tempted to wander among the statues, vases and paintings of the collection. *Bertel Thorvaldsens Plads 2. Tel: 33 32 15 32; www.thorvaldsensmuseum.dk. Open: Tue–Sun 10am–5pm. Closed: Mon. Free admission.*

Thorvaldsens Museum, backing on to a canal

Tivoli Gardens

Copenhagen's world-famous amusement garden is the country's number one tourist attraction. It lies at the heart of the city and is open for a fairytale celebration of fun and innocence throughout the summer and for a few weeks before Christmas. The gardens were founded in 1843, since when some 274 million Danes and tourists of all ages have wandered amid the thousands of blooms, the exuberant fountains, the ornamental lakes and the numerous amusements. There are merry-go-rounds, roller coasters, acrobats, musicians, dancers in fancy dress and troubadours acting out Hans Christian Andersen's stories. There are also numerous restaurants, cafés and bars.

After dark, over 100,000 lights of different colours illuminate the night sky. On Wednesdays and Saturdays, shortly before the clock strikes midnight, there is a magnificent explosion of fireworks. Then it is time to go home to bed, or alternatively, to seek out some of Copenhagen's less innocent nightlife.

One recent popular innovation is the Tivoli Christmas Market, open from late November to Christmas. Few of Tivoli's rides operate; instead the garden is full of Dickensian stalls, yuletide tableaux and other seasonal mood enhancers. *Vesterbrogade 3. Tel: 33 15 10 01; www.tivoli.com. Open: mid-Apr–mid-Sept & end Nov–Christmas, daily 11am–midnight; Hallowe'en in Tivoli 13 Oct–22 Oct 11am–9pm. Admission charge.*

IMAX Tycho Brahe Planetarium

Europe's largest planetarium stages shows on the themes of space and cosmology, as well as more terrestrial activities such as skiing and snowboarding. It is named after the famous

17th-century Danish astronomer.
Gammel Kongevej 10. Tel: 33 12 12 24;
www.tycho.dk. Open: Mon, Tue, Fri & Sat
10.30am–9pm, Wed 9.45am–9pm, Thur
9.30am–9pm, Sun 10.45am–9pm.
Admission charge.

Vor Frelsers Kirke
(Church of Our Saviour)

The unusual spire of this church, with
its exterior spiral staircase and gilt
railings, twists up to a summit crowned
by a statue of Christ standing on a
golden orb. The 400-step ascent is
rewarded by a 360-degree panorama,
and perhaps a bout of vertigo. The 17th-
century church interior has a beautifully
carved organ façade.
Skt Annæ Gade. Tel: 32 57 27 98;
www.vorfrelserskirke.dk.
Church open: Apr–Aug 11am–4.30pm;
Sept–Mar 11am–3.30pm.
Spire open: Apr–Aug 11am–4.30pm
(Sun noon–4.30pm); Sept–Oct

11am–3.30pm (Sun noon–3.30pm).
Free admission to church; admission
charge to climb the spire.

Vor Frue Kirke
(Church of Our Lady)

Copenhagen's neoclassical cathedral
stands in the heart of the Latin Quarter,
opposite the main university building,
and was reconstructed almost from
scratch in the 19th century. Of the
original building, which suffered two
major disasters, only the walls of the
side aisles and tower remain.

Even so, the cathedral is still worth a
visit, if only to see Bertel Thorvaldsen's
altar statues of Christ and the Twelve
Apostles. The font, in the form of a shell
held aloft by an angel, was also sculpted
by Thorvaldsen.
Frue Plads. Tel: 33 15 10 78;
www.koebenhavnsdomkirke.dk.
Open: Mon–Sat 7.30am–5pm, Sun
8am–7pm. Free admission.

Elaborate roller coaster at the Tivoli Gardens

Walk: Copenhagen

This pilgrimage to the compassionate Little Mermaid, who is believed to grant absolution, starts in the centre of Copenhagen and weaves through the old town to the quayside (*see map on pp22–3*).
Allow 2 hours.

Start on the Rådhuspladsen (Town Hall Square), hub of Copenhagen's bus network and effectively the centre of the city.

1 Rådhuset (Town Hall)

The huge rectangular town hall opened in 1903 and is where Copenhagen's political business is conducted. It is also one of the city's architectural jewels. A close look at the red-brick façade reveals countless details from Nordic mythology. The interior's main interests are Jens Olsen's extraordinary astronomical World Clock – and a climb up the tower for a great view of the city. *From the northeastern corner of the square, turn into pedestrianised Frederiksberggade. You are now on Strøget.*

2 Strøget (The Promenade)

Strøget is a continuous pedestrianised walkway, some say the longest in the world, made up of five streets linking

A home-made tank at Frihedsmuseet

Rådhusplasen with Kongens Nytorv, Copenhagen's other main square. Along the route are both fashionable shops and tourist fodder stores, enlivened by street entertainers. To the left is the Latin Quarter, so called because it is the equivalent of the university district of Paris. Some way down are **Gammel Torv and Nytorv** (Old and New Square), the medieval marketplace where one or two traders can still be seen doing business. *Strøget spills into Kongens Nytorv (King's Square).*

3 Kongens Nytorv

Three imposing old buildings look out over this square, surrounded by cobbles laid in concentric circles, like a running track. One is the old-fashioned Hotel d'Angleterre, the most prestigious place to stay in town. Another is the honey-coloured, gilt-crested **Kongelige Teater** (Royal Theatre), and the third is the 17th-century **Charlottenborg Palace**, housing the handsome **Royal Academy of Arts**. Here also is Scandinavia's oldest department store, Magasin du Nord, and in front of that one of the new Metro stations.
Continue across Kongens Nytorv and turn right along the furthest bank of the Nyhavn Canal.

4 Nyhavn

Traditional wooden schooners are moored along this tourist-filled quayside, lined with pavement cafés and restaurants.
Turn left onto Toldbodgade, roughly two-thirds of the way down Nyhavn. Follow this street until it reaches the fountain, with the main docks to the right. Turn left

into Amalienborg Plads (see p24), then right into Amaliegade, which brings you to the edge of Churchillparken.

5 Frihedsmuseet (Museum of the Danish Resistance)

This is the place to learn the story of the World War II Danish Resistance. News and other information filtered through an underground press and munitions for sabotaging railways and factories were received from Britain. It was a national effort to help thousands of Danish Jews escape to Sweden.
Walk through Churchillparken to the bridge across the moat that surrounds the Kastellet citadel, the longest-serving military barracks in Europe. Continue straight through the Kastellet grounds and cross the moat again. Climb a staircase and turn right, heading for the crowd that has probably gathered around Copenhagen's smallest tourist attraction.

6 Lille Havfrue (Little Mermaid)

If you are compelled to confess to excessive behaviour and seek absolution while in Copenhagen, here is the place to do it. This has been the role of the famous Little Mermaid ever since sailors discovered that such confession made them feel a whole lot better (*see pp30–31*).
A walk back along the quayside, where ferries depart for Oslo, Bornholm and the Baltics, brings you back to Nyhavn.

Museum of the Danish Resistance
Tel: 33 13 77 14; www.natmus.dk/frihed/.
Open: May–mid-Sept, Tue–Sat 10am–4pm, Sun 10am–5pm; mid-Sept–Apr, Tue–Sat 11am–3pm, Sun 11am–4pm.
Admission charge.

Tour: Copenhagen harbour

This water tour is an excellent way to see Copenhagen from a perspective that, at times, sharply differs from land-based sightseeing. Tours are run by Canal Tours Copenhagen (*tel: 33 13 31 05*) between April and October.
Allow about 1 hour.

Tours start from Gammel Strand (and from Nyhavn).

1 Gammel Strand

This was Copenhagen's most important quay in the Middle Ages. Until the 1950s it was also the site of a daily fish market, which explains the statue of a fishwife in traditional dress. The equestrian statue, further along the quay, is of Bishop Absalon, who effectively founded Copenhagen when he built the Christiansborg Palace (*see pp28–9*) on Slotsholmen Island across the canal.
The boats head for the open water and the Børsen building.

2 Børsen (Stock Exchange)

The Dutch Renaissance Stock Exchange building is a typical creation of Christian IV's reign (1588–1648), when gracious mansions and public buildings were scattered throughout Copenhagen. The modern Copenhagen stock exchange has moved elsewhere. To the left, as you leave the canal for the open harbour, is the Danish National Bank (Nationalbanken), a showpiece of modern architecture designed by the famous Danish architect, Arne Jacobsen.

3 Nyhavn

This is Denmark's best-known canal and the oldest part of the harbour. Its quay is lined with numerous bars, many of which evoke the days when the area was the haunt of sailors. Hans Christian Andersen lived here during two periods in Copenhagen, at Nos 18 (white) and

67 (red). The restored warehouse on the corner is a hotel and the lightship in front is a restaurant.
Back in the harbour are the Amaliehaven gardens to the left, with the Amalienborg Palace and Marmorkirken visible beyond.

4 Langelinie Park
The most famous feature of the waterside Langelinie Park is **Lille Havfrue** (The Little Mermaid, *see pp30–31*). The park's other monuments include the great Gefion fountain, inspired by the folk legend in which the Nordic goddess Gefion was promised as much land as she could plough in a night; and the polar bear, recalling the days when Greenland was a Danish possession.
Here the boat continues to the Trekroner fortress, from where it returns to the harbour.

5 Trekroner
The fortress, out in the harbour ahead, is built on an artificial island. It was used in 1801 in the battle won by Lord Nelson when Denmark became embroiled in the Napoleonic Wars.
The boat leaves the harbour opposite the entrance to the Nyhavn Canal, turning left to cruise along Christianshavn's canals.

6 Christianshavn
This district was established by King Christian IV in the 17th century as a separate town. Many of the gracious mansions and old warehouses lining the canal date from this period. Note the spire of Vor Frelsers Kirke (Church of Our Saviour – *see p39*) rising above and on the left of the old naval hospital which houses the Orlogsmuseet (Naval Museum – *see p35*).
The boat leaves the Christianshavn canal to cross the open harbour again. To the right is the Knippelsbro lifting bridge, connecting Slotsholmen with Christianshavn. You then return to Gammel Strand, passing the remains of the original Christiansborg Palace (see pp28–9) and the Thorvaldsens Museet (Thorvaldsens Museum see p37), both on the right.

Colourful paintwork at Nyhavn

Green ethics

Even the most cursory glance at Denmark will reveal signs that Danes are serious about environmental protection. In all Danish cities, for example, bicycles predominate as a means of transport; tracks are strictly for cyclists, who frequently have right of way over motor vehicles.

In the countryside also, there is plentiful evidence of pedal power on more than 6,000km (3,750 miles) of cycle paths.

Much more stark indicators of the national commitment to alternative energy sources are the regiments of windmills (aerogenerators) which add an ultra-modern quality to the landscape, particularly on the flat and windy expanses of southern Jutland, or on the island of Bornholm.

Although unsightly to some, most Danes see these wind-powered generators as evidence that they are paying more than lip service to the green ethic. Research on a serious scale continues apace to develop the technology to build large-scale generators. Tjæreborg, near Esbjerg, where a huge wind turbine dominates the surrounding landscape, is a major centre for this research.

Environmental policy is one of the chief criteria by which Danes judge their political parties. Any politically aware person you meet is likely to hold firm opinions, backed

up by statistics, on the precise nature of the environmental problems that face the nation (if not the world) and the sort of policies needed to resolve them. Acid rain, toxic chemical waste dumps and excess greenhouse gases are all mainstream political issues.

On an everyday practical level, Danes tend to be uncommonly conscientious recyclers of bottles, paper, tin cans and anything else recyclable. Vegetables grown with organic fertilisers were widely available in Denmark long before they were available in many other European countries. Likewise, toiletries made only with natural ingredients and a host of other environmentally friendly goods are easily available.

Danes are conscientiously true to a green philosophy – wind farms dot the countryside and inshore waters, and the bicycle is a popular mode of transport

The Frederiksborg Castle is an important landmark

Zealand

Sjælland

Denmark's largest and most densely populated island is subject to the powerful magnetic pull of Copenhagen. It is quite possible to treat Zealand as an extensive suburb of the metropolis and visit most of its attractions in a few days based in the capital. North Zealand, in particular, has several awesome castles and historic towns all within less than an hour's ride of the city. Long sandy beaches, albeit crowded in summer, are also within easy reach.

But that's no way to get to know Zealand. To take a closer look at the island, it is important to keep away from Copenhagen for a while. Down in the south of Zealand is where a taste of rural, sleepy Denmark can be had. By the time you cross the bridge to the smaller islands off Zealand's southern tip, you will have just about escaped the city's orbit and can enjoy the relative remoteness and wilder scenery.

Falster

Linked by bridges to Zealand and Lolland, Falster Island is something of a thoroughfare. On the eastern side of the island, away from a steady stream of summer traffic (much of it travelling between Copenhagen and the ferries to and from Germany), there are some fine sandy beaches and rolling dunes.

Naturists head for the beaches around Bøtø which are reserved for their undisturbed enjoyment.

Nykøbing, the island's main town, hibernates from autumn to spring, becoming a lively holiday resort, with rows of open-air cafés, in the summer. The other attraction is **Czarens Hus** (Czar's House), where Peter the Great stayed in 1716.

Two bridges link Falster to southern Zealand, and a further three cross from Falster to Lolland (see p51).

Beach lovers in Zealand

Zealand

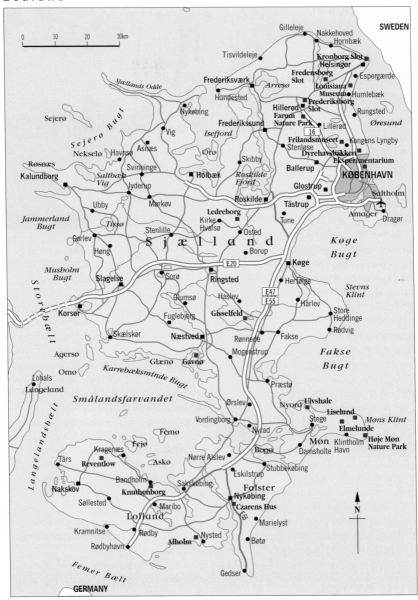

Frederiksborg Slot (Frederiksborg Castle)

Denmark's most magnificent Renaissance castle spans three small islands on the artificial Castle Lake, its spires, turrets, gables and copper-green roofs rising majestically above the town of Hillerød.

Much of the present structure was built by King Christian IV between 1602 and 1620. On ascending the throne he had the existing fortress, built by his father, Frederik II, in the previous half century, torn down. From 1671 to 1840 Frederiksborg was the home of Danish kings.

In the 18th century a catastrophic series of fires virtually razed Hillerød to the ground, destroying much of the castle. A massive restoration programme was initiated under the patronage of JC Jacobsen, the owner of Carlsberg Breweries. The result was a masterful reconstruction of the damaged sections, almost impossible to distinguish from the original parts.

The two highlights of the castle tour include the gilded **Ridder Kapellet** (Coronation Chapel), where monarchs were crowned during the two centuries when it was a royal palace, and the cavernous **Riddersalen** (Knights' Hall), with its amazingly embellished high-vaulted ceiling.

Since 1878 the castle has been Denmark's **Nationalhistoriske Museum** (Museum of National History), housing a vast collection of historical paintings, portraits, wall-sized tapestries, furniture and other antiques, displayed in endless glittering halls, chambers and corridors of gilt crystal. There are also some

Frederiksborg Castle spans three islands stretched across the placid Castle Lake

beautiful marble and carved wood panels.

There are superb views of the highly photogenic castle and its reflection in the water from the gardens on the far side of the lake.

*3400 Hillerød, 30km (19 miles) north of Copenhagen. Tel: 48 26 04 39; www.frederiksborgmuseet.dk.
Open: daily, Apr–Oct 10am–5pm; Nov–Mar 11am–3pm. Admission charge.*

Frilandsmuseet

This open-air museum, set in a beautiful wooded landscape, illustrates rural life in the 17th, 18th and 19th centuries. It houses about 100 buildings, some of them dismantled and faithfully reconstructed, stone by stone, from all over Denmark.

Many of the buildings are set in their authentic recreated environs. The coastal farm is surrounded by sand dunes and marram grass; the watermill is next to a stream. Inside are exhibits of original furniture, tools and ornaments.

The Frilandsmuseet justifies a visit of several hours, as you can follow a course through the park, building up a picture of the diversity of Danish country life in different ages, regions and social classes. *100 Kongevejen in Kongens Lyngby, 13km (8 miles) north of Copenhagen.*
Tel: 33 13 44 11; www.natmus.dk. Open: 26 Apr–Sept, Tue–Sun 10am–5pm; 1–20 Oct, Tue & Sun 10am–4pm. Admission charge.

Gilleleje

Gilleleje, at the northern tip of Zealand, dates from around 1500 and is one of Denmark's oldest fishing ports. The harbour is alive year-round with light-blue fishing boats and their catch is frequently auctioned on the quayside. In summer, this is also a humming tourist town with open-air bars and beaches nearby. A footpath leading out of town up on to the dunes makes a good walk.

The town has a small museum of local fishing and natural history, and is worth a quick visit. About 2km (1¼ miles) east, at **Nakkehoved**, is the world's first coal-fired lighthouse, built in 1772, now a small museum.
Gilleleje is 60km (37 miles) north of Copenhagen. Tourist office: Hovedgade 6F. Tel: 48 30 01 74.
Gilleleje Museum: 2 Rostgårdsvej. Tel: 48 30 16 31. Admission charge includes entry to the Nakkehoved lighthouse. Both open: mid-June–mid-Sept, 1–4pm (museum closed on Tue).

Fishing boats and pleasure craft moored alongside each other in Gilleleje's harbour

Helsingør (Elsinore)

Helsingør is a frontier town, facing Sweden across the **Øresund** – one of the world's busiest seaways, and the cause of constant commotion in the old commercial port. It grew prosperous on the 'Sound Dues' paid by every vessel which passed through between 1427 and 1857: '400 years of legal piracy' claimed some; 'The Danish King's golden egg' said the more sympathetic.

The town is best known, however, for its legendary hero Hamlet, William Shakespeare's not-quite-fictitious Prince of Denmark. The character of Hamlet was probably based on a mythological Viking figure, Amleth. Appropriately enough, Kronborg Castle, where most of the action of the play takes place, is the town's most dominant feature and it hosts an outdoor *Hamlet* production each summer.

50km (31 miles) north of Copenhagen. Tourist office: Havnepladsen 3, Box 60. Tel: 49 21 13 33.

Kronborg Slot (Kronborg Castle)

The 16th-century, four-winged Renaissance castle, built on the site of an older fortress overlooking the strategic Øresund, has been restored as a historical museum. Many visitors take a walk round the outer wall, cogitating on whether to be or not to be, before paying to go inside and explore the King's and Queen's chambers, both of

The castle of Elsinore – the setting for Shakespeare's famous play

which are richly ornamented with extravagant doorways, marble fireplaces, Flemish tapestries and ceiling paintings. The bare Great Hall, at 62m (203ft), lays claim to being Europe's longest room.

The castle also houses a separate **Handels-og Søfartsmuseet på** (Trade and Maritime Museum), charting the history of Denmark's trade and shipping through the ages.
Kronborg Slot tel: 49 21 30 78; www.kronborg.dk.
Open: May–Sept, daily 10.30am–5pm; Apr & Oct, Tue–Sun 11am–4pm; Nov–Mar, Tue–Sun 11am–3pm. Admission charge.
Handels-og Søfartsmuseet på. Tel: 49 21 06 85. Open: same hours as castle. Additional admission charge.

Hornbæk

This pretty fishing port is located near some superb beaches on the northern coast, looking across the Øresund to Kullen on a promontory jutting out of Sweden. A 200-berth marina has made it a favourite of the yachting community. It is also the starting point for the annual round-Zealand regatta in June.
12km (7 miles) northwest of Helsingør. Tourist office: Vestre Stejlebakke 2A. Tel: 49 70 47 47; www.hornbaek.dk

Kalundborg

This is the place to catch a ferry to Århus in Jutland, or to the island of Samsø. It is also worth walking round the town's small, medieval kernel to see the 12th-century **Vor Frue Kirke** (Church of Our Lady) with its five-towered spire; almost uniquely in Denmark, the church is shaped as a Greek cross. Away from the

Sunset over the dune plantation at Hornbæk

centre is the medieval **Gamle Tiendelade** (Old Tithe Barn) and the **Kalundborg og Omegns** (Museum of Kalundborg's Surroundings).
103km (64 miles) west of Copenhagen. Tourist office: Volden 12. Tel: 59 51 09 15.

Lolland Island

Denmark's third-largest island (after Zealand and Funen) is flat and sparsely populated, with great expanses of beach and an interior of extensive farmland and woods. It is linked to Falster, and thence to Zealand, by road, and to Germany via a ferry across the Femer Bælt (a bridge is due to open in 2007). Many visitors simply pass through, finding little to detain them on the island. Those with time on their hands should stop at Maribo and see the 15th-century cathedral, with its brilliant white interior and gilt altarpiece.
Lolland, south of Zealand, is linked to Falster by three road bridges (see p46).

One of Lolland Island's thatched cottages

Louisiana, Museum for Moderne Kunst (Museum of Modern Art)

A giant Henry Moore sculpture welcomes visitors to galleries set amidst landscaped parkland strewn with sculptures and huge trees. The parkland leads down to the Øresund.

The museum, with an ever-changing list of events, is internationally famous for its art exhibitions, films and concerts. Represented in the permanent exhibitions are sculptures by Alexander Calder, Jean Arp, Max Ernst and Alberto Giacometti, as well as Henry Moore; and paintings by Picasso and Warhol, as well as by prominent Danes, including Richard Mortensen, Asger Jorn, Robert Jacobsen and Carl H Petersen. Without doubt this is one of the most charming modern art museums in Europe.

Gl Strandvej 13, Humlebæk (on the Copenhagen to Helsingør coastal road, 35km (22 miles) north of the capital).
Tel: 49 19 07 19; www.louisiana.dk.
Open: Mon, Tue, Thur & Fri 10am–5pm; Wed 10am–10pm; Sat & Sun 10am–6pm. Admission charge.

Møn

Møn is by far the most beautiful of the islands south of Zealand, with its rolling green hills and the spectacular white chalk sea cliffs at **Møns Klint**. As the nearest thing Denmark has to dramatic scenery, these cliffs draw crowds all the year round. From a huge car park, trails plunge into dense woodland and along the roller-coaster cliff. It is possible to scramble down to the beach below, but be cautious.

Møn is linked by road bridge to mainland Zealand, and to Falster via the tiny island of Bogø. Tourist office: in Stege, Møn's main town, at Storegade 2.
Tel: 55 86 04 00.

Næstved

Næstved grew up around a Benedictine monastery which now houses the **Herlufen**, Denmark's most famous boarding school. Later it was a Hanseatic trading port, and today it is the largest town in south Zealand. It is also a garrison town and home to the **Gardehussar regiment** (Hussars of the Household Cavalry) who ride through the town centre amid colourful fanfare every Wednesday morning.

At other times the town has a rather sleepy air, though it has several points of interest. Næstved has two superb Gothic churches – **St Morten's**, best known for its massive altarpiece, and **St Peter's** with its richly decorated frescoes.

Næstved Museum is housed in the

Helligåndshuset (House of the Holy Spirit), a charitable institution dating from about 1400 with a good collection of medieval and modern woodcarvings.
Næstved is 80km (50 miles) southwest of Copenhagen. Tourist office: Det Gule Pakhus, Havnen 1. Tel: 55 72 11 22; www.visitnaestved.com

Ringsted

A natural crossroads in the centre of Zealand, Ringsted has a rich history as an important settlement in Viking times, and subsequently as a medieval ecclesiastical centre. Today, roads still converge on the town from all corners of the island, but its significance is mainly as an agricultural hub.

With much recent building (including shopping precincts and a new town hall), Ringsted gives the overall impression of a modern town. However, dominating the whole is the sturdy Sankt Bendts Kirke (**Saint Bendt's Church**), begun in 1160 by Valdemar the Great to house the shrine to his revered father, Knud Lavard. The shrine became a pilgrimage destination and was the burial site for Danish kings until the 14th century.

The royal tombs are the focus of the church; visit at a quiet time when the atmosphere is intensified. Particularly striking are the brass and alabaster burial slabs of Erik Menved and his wife, Queen Ingeborg.
28km (17 miles) north of Næstved. Tourist office: Sankt Bendtsgade 6. Tel: 57 62 66 00; www.ringsted.dk

Nature at its dramatic best on the isle of Møn

Roskilde

Its position on the Roskilde Fjord, giving access to the open sea, made it a prominent town in Viking times. In the 12th century Bishop Absalon made it the headquarters of the Danish Church, founding the cathedral here and effectively making it the national capital. It remained so until 1400 when the court moved to Copenhagen. Danish monarchs are still buried here.

Apart from the annual July Roskilde Festival weekend, one of Europe's largest rock-music events, most visitors come to Roskilde to visit the cathedral and the Viking Ship Museum.

30km (19 miles) west of Copenhagen. Tourist office: Gullandsstræde 15. Tel: 46 31 65 65; www.visitroskilde.com

Vikingeskibshallen (Viking Ship Museum)

Situated below the town at the edge of the Roskilde Fjord, the museum exhibits the carefully reconstructed remains of five Viking longships discovered and excavated between 1962 and 1967.

Tel: 46 30 02 00; www.vikingeskibsmuseet.dk. Open: daily, all year, 10am–5pm. Admission charge.

Domkirke (Cathedral)

The massive red-brick cathedral is one of the most impressive buildings in Denmark. Architecturally, it is also one of the most important, with extensions in different styles added over the centuries. Work started in the 1170s on the orders of Bishop Absalon, though the main structure, a mixture of Gothic and Romanesque, was not finished until

the early 1400s. The tall, thin steeples were added in the 16th century.

The interior is vast, airy and adorned with innumerable treasures and historical curiosities. Don't miss the ingenious 16th-century clock on the south wall, just above the entrance, where a mechanical St George attacks a dragon on the hour.

The main sights, however, are the royal tombs, where 20 kings and 17 queens are interred in four chapels. There is a great variety of styles amid the gilt, marble, silver and bronze – ranging from the richly ornamented chapel of Christian IV, to the simple slab marking the resting place of Frederik IX, father of the present queen.

Domkirkestræde 10. Tel: 46 31 65 65; www.roskildedomkirke.dk. Open: Apr–Sept, Mon–Sat 9am–4.45pm, Sun 12.30–4.45pm; Oct–Mar, Tue–Sat 10am–3.45pm, Sun 12.30–3.45pm. From mid-June–mid-Aug there are guided tours in English. Admission charge.

Rungsted

The **Karen Blixen Museet** (Museum), dedicated to the life of the novelist and traveller (1885–1962), is the reason to stop at Rungsted. The large country house was her childhood home to which she returned in 1931 to write *Out of Africa* and other works. She died here in 1962 and is buried in a movingly simple grave under a beech tree in the grounds.

A tour of the house takes in the rooms where Blixen lived and wrote. There is also an exhibition of photographs spanning her life, including many taken in Africa. A 16-ha (40-acre) park is now a bird sanctuary.

Rungsted is on the 152N coastal road, 20km (12 miles) south of Helsingør. Karen Blixen Museet: Strandvej 111, Rungsted Kyst. Tel: 45 57 10 57; www.karen-blixen.dk. Open: May–Sept, Tue–Sun 10am–5pm; Oct–Apr, Wed–Fri 1–4pm, Sat & Sun 11am–4pm. Admission charge.

Vordingborg

Vordingborg is an old market town and port, much of which has been rebuilt in recent years, giving it a modern aspect. Since the town is linked by bridge to Møn, many motorists pass through it on their way to the island. The main attraction is the **Gasetårn** (Goose Tower), the only surviving corner of a 14th-century wall which once surrounded a massive castle, now in ruins. The tower was said to have once been crowned by a gilded goose as a calculated insult to Hanseatic traders. If you climb it you will be rewarded with commanding views over the town and across to Møn.

Vordingborg is at the southwestern tip of Zealand, opposite the island of Falster. Tourist office: Algade 96. Tel: 55 34 11 11; www.visitvordingborg.dk

Floating exhibits at the Viking Ship Museum, Roskilde

Tour: North Zealand

This car tour winds a leisurely way along some of North Zealand's minor roads and winding lanes, crossing humpback bridges and tracing the shores of lakes and fjords. Much of the tour is on the 'Marguerite Route' (*see* Driving, *p180*), and it skirts several major attractions described elsewhere in this section.

Allow about 5 hours.

From central Copenhagen follow signs for the 152N coastal road, which is also signposted as the Marguerite Route. Just past the upmarket suburb of

Charlottenlund, the metropolis comes to an end with Bellevue beach on the right and the Dyrehave, at Klampenborg, on the left.

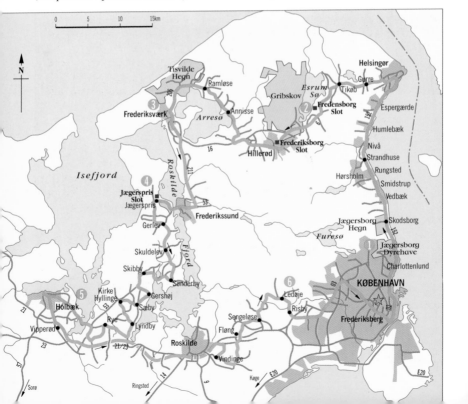

1 Jægersborg Dyrehave

Denmark's oldest deer park has been preserved as an expanse of open land and broad-leafed forest, covering more than 1,000 undulating hectares (2,471 acres). It is a glorious place to stretch your legs or, for the less energetic, to spot deer from the horse-drawn carriages that are for hire.

Continue north along the 152. As you reach Helsingør (see p50), take the Marguerite Route left towards Hillerød, stopping at Fredensborg Slot (castle).

2 Fredensborg Slot

Also known as 'The Palace of Peace', this summer residence of the Danish royal family is spectacularly located on the edge of Esrum Sø (lake). Completed in 1776, its style is more that of a country house than a defensive castle. Parts of the palace are open to the public at restricted times in summer, but the real treat is to wander the lakeside gardens that are open all year.

Continue along the Marguerite Route, passing Hillerød (see p48) to the left, before curving round the northern end of Arresø (lake) to Frederiksværk.

3 Frederiksværk

Stop at the town to walk along the canal towpath connecting Arresø Lake (Denmark's largest) with the **Roskilde Fjord**, which leads to the open sea. The town grew up around this canal.

The Marguerite Route traces the eastern side of the boat-dotted Roskilde Fjord, with farmland and paddocked horses to the right. At Frederikssund turn right for the bridge over the fjord, following the route round to Jægerspris Slot.

4 Jægerspris Slot

This superb castle, set in fine gardens, probably dates back to the 11th century, but was completely rebuilt by Frederik VII, who acquired it in 1854 and died there in 1863.

Continue along the Marguerite Route, twisting through hidden backwaters and medieval villages away from the main road, as far as Holbæk.

5 Holbæk

Fjord-side Holbæk is one of the most ancient towns in Zealand, starting first as a port and later becoming the seat of a Dominican priory. While exploring the backstreets and half-timbered houses, do not miss the excellent museum that illustrates the development of the town and surrounding area.

Join the main 21 road eastwards towards Roskilde (see p54), rejoining the Marguerite Route immediately east of the town. Follow the route to Ledøje.

6 Ledøje

This small village has one of the most unusual churches in Denmark. Built with one storey for commoners and one for the gentry, the 13th-century building is effectively two churches sharing a single altar.

Follow the Marguerite Route back into central Copenhagen.

Jægerspris Slot
Tel: 47 53 10 04; www.kongfrederik.dk. Open: 7 Apr–28 Oct, Tue–Sun 11am–3pm (guided tours in English).
The Museum of Holbæk
Klosterstræde. Tel: 59 43 23 53; www.holbmus.dk. Open: Tue–Fri 10am–4pm; Sat & Sun, noon–4pm. Closed: Jan.

Bornholm

This small island out in the Baltic, 180km (112 miles) east of Zealand, has become one of Denmark's most popular tourist resorts. Expanses of beach, dramatically rocky headlands, formidable ruined castles, rolling pastures, fairytale woodland, whitewashed churches, huddled harbours and quaint, gaily painted villages of half-timbered cottages, all help to make it irresistible to the lover of peace and tranquillity.

Typical, gaily painted houses in Bornholm

Tourism to Bornholm received a welcome shot in the arm with the introduction of a rail service across the new Øresund bridge, linking to a ferry from Sweden. Travel time from Copenhagen to Bornholm is three hours, instead of the earlier half-day ferry ride it once took.

In Bornholm there are more than 200km (124 miles) of winding cycle paths to explore. The island is a joy for relaxed cyclists and also perfect for keen hikers and trekkers.

Bornholm

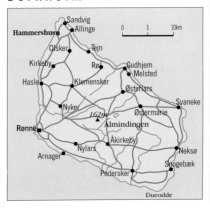

Peace in this idyll has not been easily won, however. Its strategic position in the Baltic has led to Bornholm being fought over for centuries, most recently in 1945 when the commandant of the occupying Germans refused to surrender despite capitulation to the Allies. The Russians responded by bombing **Rønne** and **Neksø**, the two main towns, then occupying the island themselves for several months before restoring Danish sovereignty. During the Cold War Bornholm was one of NATO's key surveillance bases.

Islanders do not want their hard-fought way of life to be diluted by unfettered tourism. Consequently there are special laws that help keep the island communities alive including one forbidding any foreigner from buying land. Others restrict the use of homes as holiday properties. Strict monitoring of air and ferry tickets ensures that the total number of visitors never exceeds the resident population of around 44,000 at any one time, although the area receives nearly 450,000 tourists over the summer.

Åkirkeby

In the Middle Ages, when pirates and other enemies at sea kept population centres away from the coast, this inland town was the most important on Bornholm, with the island's regional council meeting here until 1776.

It was also the ecclesiastical centre, with the island's most unusual church, whose thickset 12th-century walls suggest that, like many other Bornholmer churches, it also served a defensive purpose. There is a fine late Romanesque porch, decorated with rune stones, and a superb baptismal font carved from stone.

12km (7 miles) east of Rønne.
Tourist office: Torvet 2.
Tel: 56 97 45 20.

Christiansø

From Gudhjem, Svaneke or Allinge (near the north tip of Bornholm) you can take a ferry across about 17km (11 miles) of water to Christiansø or **Frederiksø**, the largest in a tiny archipelago of Danish specks in the Baltic that together support about 130 people. A third, **Græsholm**, is a protected bird sanctuary. The islands were fortified by Christian V and played an important role in the Napoleonic Wars, when attacks on the British fleet were launched from here.

Christiansø lies 20km (12 miles) to the east of Bornholm.

Dueodde

Dueodde is Bornholm's best beach area, with rolling dunes and endless stretches

Sleepy Åkirkeby was once Bornholm's key town

of sand so fine that, in bygone days, it used to be exported all over Europe as 'writing sand' to sprinkle over and absorb wet ink. The beach shelves so gently into the sea that, in places, the tide comes in and out as fast as you can walk. In the opposite direction, the dunes lead into sandy pine woodlands dotted with holiday cottages. There are also several campsites.

There is no village to Dueodde – just a hotel, café and bus stop, and a lighthouse which opens to the public at irregular times.

20km (12 miles) southeast of Rønne.

Gudhjem

The main street leading down from a rocky headland to Gudhjem is so steep that cyclists are required by law to dismount. Fig trees and vines, climbing up the red-tiled cottages huddled round the two harbours, lend the little port a Mediterranean air. Movie buffs might recognise one of the settings for the Oscar-winning *Pelle the Conqueror*, based on Martin Andersen Nexø's novel on the miserable life of 19th-century Swedish immigrants.

Today, Gudhjem is best known for its herring smokehouses. Here you can watch as fresh fish are gutted, dried in the wind and hung in a chimney while men use damp sacking on the end of sticks to beat the flames down and keep the smoke from billowing. Some say that this technique was taught to Gudhjem fishermen by Scottish soldiers stationed on Christiansø. Whatever the truth, a visit to Gudhjem should be rounded off

Bornholm's round churches once also served as strongholds and observation posts

with a meal of these 'Golden Bornholmers', still warm from the smokery; they are delicious served with black rye bread, coarse sea salt and strong Danish beer.

The small museum in the abandoned railway station is worth a visit for its collection of local art.
19km (12 miles) northeast of Rønne.
Tourist office: Åbogade 9.
Tel: 56 48 52 10.
Museum open: mid-May–mid-Sept, Mon–Sat 10am–4pm, Sun 2–5pm.

Hammershus

The massive, ruined castle of Hammershus perches dramatically at the edge of the island's 75-m (246-ft) high northwestern cliff. Historians disagree about the castle's origins, though few dispute that it was once the greatest fortress in northern Europe. It was probably built in the 13th century, during the struggle between the Danish Crown and the Church. Since Bornholm was so vital for control of the Baltic, the castle changed hands many times, and was expanded by many rulers. It was severely damaged by artillery when Bornholm was captured by Sweden in 1645. Thirteen years later the people of Bornholm revolted against the Swedes and the castle was never again used as a fortress. It later became a prison, then a garrison, before falling into disrepair.

The best way to experience the overall scale of the castle is to walk all the way around the ring wall that encircles it. A bridge from the eastern side gives access to the castle ruins.

Lines of smoked herring drying in Gudhjem

20km (12 miles) north of Rønne.
Unrestricted access to the castle ruins all
year round.

Melsted

Tiny Melsted is worth a visit for the
agricultural museum housed in the
17th-century Melstedgård farm. This is a
'living museum' where the traditional
agricultural methods of the island are
demonstrated. There are also various
exhibits on farming life through the
ages, with tableaux and original
implements.
1km (⅔ mile) south of Gudhjem, 18km
(11 miles) northeast of Rønne.
Melstedgård Agricultural Museum:
Melstedvej 25. Tel: 56 48 55 98;
www.bornholmsmuseer.dk.
Open: mid-May–mid-Sept, Tue–Sun
10am–5pm. Admission charge.

Neksø

On Bornholm's east coast, Neksø is the
island's second-largest town, although
the population is barely 4,000. The
harbour, however, is out of all
proportion to the rest of the port, busy
with the constant toing and froing of
fishing boats and with the cry of
seabirds filling the air. Although Neksø
was bombed by the Russians in 1945,
parts of the old centre, characterised by
sandstone-walled houses, have survived.
25km (16 miles) east of Rønne.
Neksø-Dueodde tourist office: Sdr.
Hammer 2A. Tel: 56 49 70 79.

Østerlars

The thickset circular church at Østerlars
is the largest and best known of several
on Bornholm that were built not just as
places of worship but also as lookout

The ruins of Hammershus Castle

posts and a last line of defence for villagers against whatever enemies might be lurking offshore. Seven massive buttresses support the walls, rising three storeys high, which can be climbed via narrow interior staircases. Narrow slit windows offer commanding views over the island and the grey sea beyond the shores.

17km (11 miles) northeast of Rønne. Østerlars Kirke: Gudhjemsvej 28. Open: Apr–Oct, Mon–Sat 9am–5pm. Admission charge.

Rønne

With a population of about 15,000, Rønne is Bornholm's main town and capital. The 1945 Russian bombing left few parts of the town intact, but many of the narrow streets of cross-timbered houses, painted bright yellow, orange

and blue, have been carefully rebuilt, contributing to the atmosphere of an oversized village.

There is a large harbour where fishing boats and ferries dock. The town also has a yachting marina and, nearby, some good beaches.

Rønne's tourist office which is also the main one for the island is the Bornholms Velkomstcenter, Ndr Kystvej 3. Tel: 56 95 95 00; www.bornholm.info

Bornholm Museum

This is the place to study the history and prehistory of Bornholm. Among the finds is a collection of Roman gold and silver coins unearthed on the island. There are also some beautiful paintings by Bornholmer artists, capturing the light and essence of the island, and displays of ceramics by several of the island's famous potters.

Laksegade 7. Tel: 56 95 07 35; www.bornholmsmuseer.dk. Open: mid-May–mid-Sept, Mon–Sat 10am–5pm. Admission charge.

Svaneke

This picturesque little port of 1,200 people nestling within a cove on the island's rocky northeastern coast is a splash of colour with its bright, limewashed and half-timbered houses. It is also one of the smallest market towns in Denmark, with a charter dating back more than 400 years. The whole village has been declared a conservation area since 1968 and has since won awards for its sensitive preservation.

20km (12 miles) east of Rønne. Tourist office: Storegade 24. Tel: 56 49 63 50.

By bike: Bornholm

This ride through Bornholm's undulating interior takes in the island's beautiful scenery, as well as some unexpected surprises along the way.

Allow 3 hours.

1 Rønne

Bikes are the main form of transport in the town, with cycle tracks lining all the main streets (*see p63*). Islanders and holidaymakers can be seen on an extraordinary variety of two-wheeled contraptions, going about their business with bells ringing, or setting off for a day in the countryside.

Take the signposted cycle track towards Lobbæk, which follows the bed of the disused Rønne-Neksø railway line. After about 4km (2½ miles), stop at the village of Nylars, and look out for the traditional round church on the left.

2 Nylars Rundkirke (Nylars Round Church)

This is a perfect example of the round, white-walled churches that are sprinkled around Bornholm. Like several others on the island, it was built in the troubled 12th century and was as much a defensive bastion as a place of worship. In 1335 it was dedicated to the patron saint of seafarers, St Nicholas. Note the

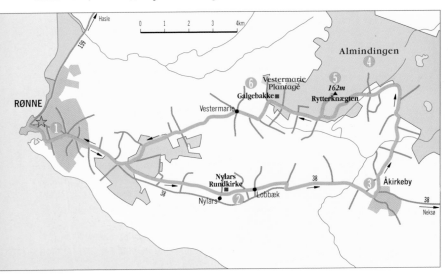

circular central pillar which is beautifully decorated with a frieze. *Continue to the village of Lobbæk. Here you leave the former railway, but stay on the cycle track that continues through fields dotted with aerogenerators, then follows the metalled road from Rønne to Åkirkeby. About 5km (3 miles) on from Lobbæk, you enter Åkirkeby.*

3 Åkirkeby
See p59.
Follow the signposted cycle track north from the village, towards Almindingen and Gudhjem. You soon plunge into a forest.

4 Almindingen
Almindingen, meaning 'The Common', is the third-largest forest in Denmark – covering 24sq km (9sq miles) of the island's hilliest ground. It was cleared in the 17th century as a public grazing area for cattle, but later replanted with a mixture of deciduous and coniferous trees. This is the most enchanting part of the day's ride, as the path meanders past marshy ponds alive with noisily croaking frogs.
Follow a signpost to the right, which leads steadily up a track to Rytterknægten, an iron-girder tower rising out of the forest.

5 Rytterknægten
The tower marks the highest point on the island, and the third-highest in the whole of Denmark. Climbing up the tower provides an unexpected reminder of Bornholm's strategic location between the east and the west. As you leave the treetops behind, an array of aerials, dishes, receivers and all kinds of surveillance equipment emerges from

It is the bicycle that reveals the essential Denmark

leafy hiding places. A stark sign warns you not to take photographs.
Return to the main Rønne-Gudhjem cycle track and follow it towards Rønne, stopping after 1.5km (1 mile) at the Vestermarie Plantage.

6 Vestermarie Plantage (Plantation)
This is one of the most fascinating archaeological sites on Bornholm, with several points of interest within a very short distance of each other. Just south of the cycle track are some fine Bronze Age carved-stone ships; nearby is a distinctive mound, known as **Galgebakke**, believed to have been a place of execution. Beside the mound is a dense collection of cairns, marking the burial site of urns containing cremated human remains.
Continue along the cycle track back towards Rønne. Shortly before the town, it rejoins the Rønne-Åkirkeby track along the disused railway.

Linking Copenhagen

July 1 2000, when Queen Margrethe cut the ribbon to officially open the spectacular Øresund Fixed Link tunnel and bridge, it heralded a new era of Scandinavian co-operation. The 16-km (10-mile) road and rail link from Copenhagen's Kastrup Airport to Sweden's third-largest city, Malmø, was not just an awesome feat of engineering prowess, but a social and cultural link that has already reaped dividends for the inhabitants of the new, so-called Øresund region (encompassing the eastern coast of Zealand, Copenhagen and southern Sweden). For visitors this means that with Malmø just 35 minutes away by train from Copenhagen's Central Station, they can visit two countries in one holiday.

Malmø is a delightful, historic city, far smaller than Copenhagen, but arguably even more attractive, with beautiful parks and a long, sandy beach called Ribban. Its café squares have a more Mediterranean feel, and the city has a younger, more ethnically diverse population than Copenhagen (thanks to Sweden's more lenient immigration laws

and the two universities in the area). Besides, shopping here tends to be cheaper for non-Danes.

But the Øresund bridge has not been a complete success in terms of traffic. High road tolls have dissuaded many from driving across the bridge and the consortium behind the project has had to revise its budget.

Happily, the even larger, 18-km (11-mile) long Storebælts Broen (The Great Belt Bridge) linking the Danish island of Fyn to western Zealand has been more of a success since it opened in 1997, despite its equally high tariffs.

Since Denmark comprises more than 400 islands, bridges such as the Øresund (left) and The Great Belt (above) play a crucial role in uniting the country politically and socially

Funen

Fyn

Green as a croquet lawn, the country's second-largest island is often called the 'Garden of Denmark'. The term is thought to have been used first by Hans Christian Andersen, who was born in the island's capital, Odense. Funen's gently rolling hills, luxuriant pastures, broad-leaved forests and winding lanes were a source of inspiration to the great poet and author of many well-loved fairy stories.

A sign in Ærøskøbing, on Ærø

The same notions of flowing magical beauty are to be found in the works of fellow islander Carl Nielsen, Denmark's foremost composer. He is said to have believed that the lilting local accent was an expression of a rare musicality among the people of Funen.

Funen is joined to Jutland by a bridge spanning the Lillebælt and by the **Great Belt Fixed Link** to Zealand (*see p67*). The Great Belt, in particular, has done much to dispel insularity and integrate Funen with the rest of the country. Even so, the main city Odense still gives the impression of an oversized village.

To the south is an archipelago of smaller islands, reached from the port of Svendborg, with an even stronger aura of calm and isolation. Langeland and Ærø, in particular, are excellent for cycling.

Ærø

By far the largest of Funen's islands not to be connected by bridge, Ærø is the jewel of the archipelago. Holidaymakers boarding ferries from Svendborg or Fåborg are lured by the gentle green hills topped with windmills and strewn with prehistoric burial mounds, as well as the abundant bird life, beaches, idyllic fishing ports and farming hamlets. Few bother to bring their cars – Ærø is ideal hiking and biking country.
12km (7 miles) south of Fåborg. Ærø Tourist office: Vestergade 1, Ærøskøbing. Tel: 62 52 13 00; www.arre.dk

Ærøskøbing

Impossibly pretty, Ærø's romantic main town of Ærøskøbing consists of half-timbered cottages lime-washed in a spectrum of colours, interspersed with larger bow-windowed houses. This is the only town in Denmark preserved by law, making it into a town-sized museum.

The squares and cobbled alleys are littered with curiosities, such as ancient wooden water pumps, and the oldest post office in Denmark (dating from 1749). The **Ærø Museum** (*Brogade 3–5, tel: 62 52 29 50*) charts the history of the island, and the **Flaskeskibssamlingen** (*Smedgade 22, tel: 62 52 29 51*) has a vast collection of bottle-ships.

Funen

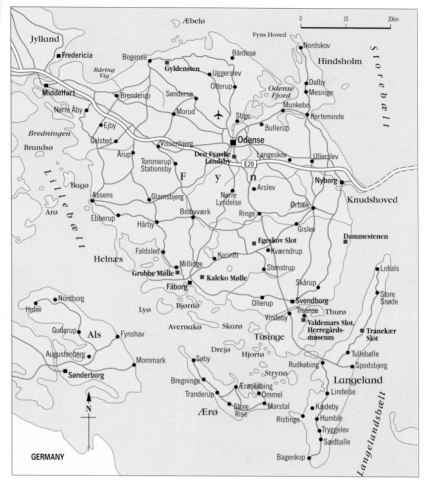

Ærøskøbing is on the northern coast of Ærø.

Assens

An enchanting little fishing port, yachting centre and holiday town on the Lillebælt, Assens comprises an old town of gabled merchants' houses and a busy modern shopping centre.

The chief attraction is '**De 7 Haver**', with seven gardens laid out to represent different horticultural traditions.
39km (24 miles) southwest of Odense.
Idéhaven 'De 7 Haver': Aa-Strandvej
Ebberup 33. Tel: 64 74 12 85.
Open: mid-Apr–Oct, daily 10am–6pm.
Admission charge.

Egeskov Slot (Egeskov Castle)

Standing in the middle of a lake, like a giant ship at anchor, this soaring, surrealistically pink and turreted castle is one of Denmark's most famous landmarks. It is a rare example of a Danish national monument privately owned by an aristocratic family. No visit to Funen is complete without seeing Egeskov, and the owners have gone to great lengths to make this one of the country's premiere family attractions.

Visitors cross a drawbridge to reach the interior, where the rooms are themed on different eras in the castle's 440-year history. White walls give it an airy feel as you wander, alone or with a guide, from the Louis XVI Gule Stue (Yellow Room) to the 19th-century Klunkestuen (Victorian Room) and through many other chambers exquisitely furnished with period pieces. Most striking are the Jagtstuen (Hunting Room) and Jagtgangen (Hunting Corridor), hung with thousands of African big-game trophies shot by a former owner in the last century.

Peacocks strut and flags flutter in the surrounding gardens where a motor museum, with a fine collection of carriages, cars, motorcycles and aircraft, fills various outhouses. There is also a maze and a large children's playground. *27km (17 miles) south of Odense, at Egeskovgade 18 Kværndrup. Tel: 62 27 10 16; www.egeskov.com. Open: daily, May*

The dreamlike Egeskov Castle seems to have been transported straight out of a fairytale

& Sept 10am–5pm; June & Aug 9am–6pm
(castle 10am–5pm); July 10am–7pm
(castle 10am–7pm). Admission charge.

Fåborg

Looking out across the sea from
southwestern Funen to some of the
smallest islands of the archipelago, this
delightful little jewel of a town is also an
important ferry hub with connections to
Ærø, Als and Gelting (in Germany), and
to tiny Lyø, Avernakø and Bjørnø.

A busy waterfront road hides a maze
of back alleys, archways, cobbles and
photogenic streets, particularly
Tårngade, lined with old merchants'
houses and hung with flowers. On the
hour, a carillon chimes hymn tunes
from the belfry high above.
37km (23 miles) south of Odense.

Fåborg Museum

This is the place to view the works of the
famous Funen Painters' school of
landscape artists, which flourished from
1890 to 1920. Peter Hansen, Fritz Syberg
and Johannes Larsen were the leading
lights of the era, and this is the most
extensive collection of their work
anywhere in the world. Those who have
already slowed down to the gentle pace
of Funen's rural life, to enjoy its bright
colours and feel the breeze rustling in
the oak forests, will appreciate how
superbly this trio captures the island's
atmosphere.

Also on display are the works of local
sculptors, including the renowned Kai
Nielsen, and some Funen furniture.
*Grønnegade 75. Tel: 62 61 06 65;
www.faaborgmuseum.dk. Open: Tue–Sun,
June–Aug 10am–5pm; Apr, May, Sept &*

The Old Merchant's House, now a museum,
recalls Fåborg's glorious trading days

---

*Oct 10am–4pm; Nov–Mar 11am–3pm.
Closed: Mon. Admission charge.*

Gamle Gaard (Old Merchant's House)

This 1725 house contains a series of
evocative tableaux recreating town life in
the 18th and 19th centuries, when
Fåborg was an important and
prosperous trading post, with one of the
largest merchant fleets in Denmark. The
sumptuous master bedroom, the kitchen
and the beautifully planted garden
featuring a summer pavilion all
demonstrate the enormous opulence
seen in Fåborg during those centuries.
*Holkegade 1. Tel: 62 61 33 38.
Open: mid-May–mid-Sept, daily
10.30am–4.30pm. Admission charge.*

Flat and green Langeland is a popular family resort

Kerteminde

Johannes Larsen, among the foremost of the Funen Painters (*see p71*), described this as 'the prettiest little town in the world, lying there deep in the bay by the mouth of the fjord'. Hyperbole, of course, but Kerteminde is the very epitome of a Danish fishing village, with half-timbered houses, tarred huts, narrow cobbled alleys and a harbour abob with fishing boats – no matter that nowadays most of them take anglers out on day trips, and that the whole town has been sanitised for tourism. Larsen's birthplace has been converted into a bright, colourful little museum of local culture with a collection of his work.
22km (14 miles) east of Odense. Johannes Larsen Museum: Møllebakken. Tel: 65 32 11 77. Open: Tue–Sun 10am–4pm. Admission charge.

Langeland

Long, spindly Langeland is one of the most popular islands in the Funen archipelago for sea and sand holidays; many families have summer houses here, and there are several campsites. Although frequently windswept, the island's beaches are backed by sand dunes and speckled with marram grass which offers shelter if necessary. It is a prime location for windsurfing.

Away from the beaches and dunes, fertile Langeland is divided into neat fields of arable land and dairy pasture. At **Tranekær** a red fairytale castle rises out of the landscape (closed to the public, although the gardens and a windmill in the grounds can be visited). There is a good network of cycle tracks.

The main town is **Rudkøbing**, with its characterful old fishing port of half-timbered houses and cobbled lanes, as well as a modern yachting marina lined with open-air cafés. The **Langeland Museum** specialises in prehistoric and Viking finds from the island. **Det Gamle Apotek** (The Old Apothecary) has a collection of old pharmacists' paraphernalia.
Langeland, lying southeast of Fyn (Funen), is reached by road from Funen, via the island of Tåsinge, by ferry from Fåborg via the island of Ærø, and by road from Fåborg.
Langeland Museum: Jens Winthersvej. Tel: 63 51 10 10. Open: Mon–Thur 10am–4pm, Fri 10am–1pm. Admission charge.
Det Gamle Apotek: Brogade 15. Tel: 63 51 10 10. Open: mid-June–Aug, Mon–Fri 11am–4pm. Admission charge.

Nyborg

Nyborg's strategic position, on the narrowest part of the **Storebælt**, has ensured its prosperity since the 12th century, when an indomitable castle was constructed here to guard the Storebælt. The ancient castle and the Storebælt project's exhibition centre represent the glorious juxtaposition of Denmark old and new.

Nyborg is 31km (19 miles) east of Odense.

Nyborg Slot (Nyborg Castle)

This was the greatest of a string of defensive castles built along the Storebælt in the 12th and 13th centuries. It became a royal palace where various kings resided until 1620 when ferocious storms and, subsequently, bombardment during the 1658–60 war with Sweden badly damaged it. Deemed no longer suitable for royalty, the castle fell into decay.

Restoration has been meticulous, with tours today capturing the medieval aura in the sparse and echoing Great Hall, and the Danehof Hall, where the ancient parliament used to meet.

Slotsgade 11, DK5800 Nyborg.
Tel: 65 31 02 07; www.museer-nyborg.dk.
Open: July, Tue–Sun 10am–5pm; Aug & June, Tue–Sun 10am–4pm; Mar–May, Sept & Oct, Tue–Sun 10am–3pm.
Admission charge.

Nyborg Castle has been meticulously restored to its medieval glory

Odense

Hans Christian Andersen himself welcomes visitors to the city of his birth. His pointed-nose profile flutters on thousands of bunting flags along the main shopping streets. In top hat and tail coat he is seen leading a troupe of fellow actors dressed as schoolchildren, in open-air productions of his fairytales. His ubiquity extends to statues, hotels and cafés bearing his name, books, cassettes and posters on him, and two museums dedicated to his life and works – the main museum was expanded to commemorate his 200th birth anniversary in 2005. (*See pp78–9 for more details on Andersen.*)

HC Andersen's characters dot the town of Odense

Before getting to grips with Andersen-mania, it is worth remembering that Odense was an important city centuries before the great fairytale author was born. Odense means 'Odin's Shrine', referring to the Norse god of war. As the site of King Knud's murder, and later canonisation, the cathedral attracted Christian pilgrims throughout the Middle Ages. Later, with the building of a canal to Kerteminde on the Storebælt, Odense became an important commercial town. It remains Denmark's third-largest city (after Copenhagen and Århus) and the administrative centre of Funen, despite an unhurried provincial atmosphere.

Several good museums testify to the richness of Odense's history, and most of the attractions are within easy walking distance of each other. With parks, open spaces and a river running through the town, Odense is airy, and relaxing, although the overall aspect is marred by unsightly modern office blocks. As a university town it is lively during term time, and has many late-night cafés. *Tourist office: Vestergade 2. Tel: 66 12 75 20; www.odenseturist.dk*

Brandts Klædefabrik (Brandt's Cloth Mill)

This former textile factory has been converted into an arts centre with a fast turnover of exhibitions in the bright and spacious shop floors once used for spinning and weaving. The emphasis in the main Kunsthallen (Art Gallery) is on up-and-coming international talent in the visual arts, sculpture, architecture, design and handicrafts. There is also the **Museet for Fotokunst** (Museum of Photographic Art), with its collection of classical photography as well as changing modern exhibitions; and the **Danmarks Grafiske Museum** (Danish Museum of Printing), charting the development of printing in Denmark over the past three centuries. *Brandts Passage 37. Tel: 65 91 19 42;*

www.tidenssamling.dk. Open: July & Aug, daily 10am–5pm, otherwise Tue–Sun. Admission charge.

Carl Nielsen Museet (Carl Nielsen Museum)

Appropriately enough, this homage to the life of Denmark's foremost composer is located inside Odense's magnificent concert hall, the largest in Denmark.

The museum traces Nielsen's life and career through photographs, original scores and extracts from both his early and his later, more famous pieces, played through headphones. There are also selected examples from his writings, such as *Springtime in Funen* and *My Childhood* – memoirs from his early years on the island. Nielsen's wife, Anne Marie, was a well-known sculptor and several of her works enliven the museum. *Claus Bergs Gade 11. Tel: 66 12 00 57, ext 4671; www.museum.odense.dk. Open: Jan–Aug, Thur–Sun noon–4pm; Sept–Dec, Thur & Fri 4–8pm, Sun & holidays noon–4pm. Admission charge.*

Odense town plan (*see pp82–3 for walk route*)

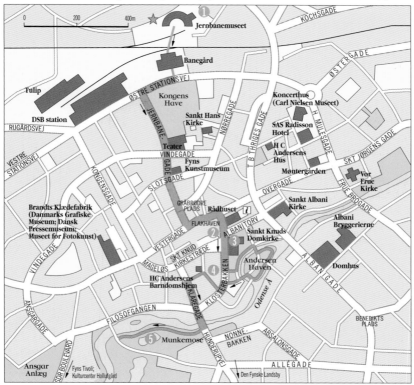

Fynske Landsby (Funen Village)

A smithy, a cobbler's workshop, a village school, a watermill, a windmill, a merchant's house, workers' cottages, a prison house, a duck pond, farm animals and cobbled streets are just a few of the exhibits which make up this convincing display of life in a typical Funen village in the 18th and 19th centuries.

People in period costumes work at their crafts. Cattle-raising and agriculture are practised with the original methods. In other exhibitions, there are life-size figures in authentic period costumes. Many of the tools, artefacts and ornaments are genuine period pieces.

Sejerskovvej 20. Tel: 65 51 46 01; www.museum.odense.dk. Open: Apr–mid-June, Tue–Sun 10am–5pm; mid-June–mid-Aug, daily 9.30am–7pm; mid-Aug–Oct, Tue–Sun 10am–5pm; Nov–Mar, Sun & holidays 11am–3pm. Admission charge.

HC Andersen's Hus (Hans Christian Andersen's House)

You've heard his fairytales; now discover the man (*see pp78–9*). This is the main museum devoted to the writer's life, converted from several houses knocked together, including the one in which Andersen was supposedly born in 1805 (though there is no documentary evidence to support this claim).

Pre-industrial life on show at Fynske Landsby

Since he was such a great hoarder of correspondence and personal effects, there is plenty for the serious Andersenologist to sift through – letters, photographs and original manuscripts of his work, which he wrote in several languages. Maps chart his many European travels, together with the voluminous trunks he took with him and a case containing his famous black top hat. A length of rope is also displayed – he is said to have taken it with him everywhere as a means of escape out of a fear of fire.

The circular central hall is splashed with murals illustrating Andersen's life, and, in a separate library, there is a huge collection of tomes of his work, in 70 different languages. There is also a collection of illustrations by Andersen himself, and by other artists inspired by his stories. A large extension to mark the 200th anniversary of Andersen's birth opened in 2005, while next door **Fyrtøjet**, a new museum aimed at children and play, has also opened.

This museum should not be confused with the HC Andersen's Barndomshjem on Munkemøllestræde (*see p83*), Andersen's home from the age of two, where there is a small exhibition illustrating his childhood.
Bangs Boder 29. Tel: 65 51 46 01;
www.museum.odense.dk. Open: mid-
June–Aug, daily 9am–7pm; Sept–mid-June,
Tue–Sun 10am–4pm. Admission charge.
Fyrtøjet (Children's Culture House):
Hans Jensens Stræde 21. Tel: 66 14 44 11;
www.museum.odense.dk. Open: Feb–Dec,
Tue–Sat 11am–4pm. Fairytale reading
daily 2pm (Sat at noon). Puppet show
Tue–Fri at 3pm. Admission charge.

Møntergården (Museum of Cultural and Urban History)

This museum, in a run of adjoining 16th- and 17th-century half-timbered houses, is far less dry than its name suggests. Odense's pre-Andersen era is brought imaginatively to life through a chronological series of life-size tableaux, backed up by archaeological finds such as coins, medals and tools. The town's history is covered since the days of the Vikings, through medieval craftsmen, to the work of the Dominican friars.
Overgade 48. Tel: 65 51 46 01;
www.museum.odense.dk.
Open: Tue–Sun 10am–4pm.
Admission charge. Closed for renovation –
due to re-open 2007.

Sankt Knuds Domkirke (Saint Canute's Cathedral)

This is one of Denmark's major cathedrals, a vast Gothic structure built in the 13th century. Its bright, airy, whitewashed and frescoed interior hides some architectural and spiritual treasures which are often ignored in a city that is more focused on fairytales and modern art.

Be sure not to miss the magnificent gold and woodcarved altarpiece, or the worn steps down to the tombs of Saint Canute and Saint Alban. (Some experts believe that the latter may actually contain the remains of Canute's brother, Benedict.)
Sankt Knud Kirkestræde.
Tel: 66 12 03 92.
Open: Apr–Oct, Mon–Sat 9am–5pm &
Sun noon–5pm; Nov–Mar, Mon–Sat
10am–4pm & Sun noon–5pm.
Free admission.

Hans Christian Andersen

Once upon a time, in a tumbledown cottage at Odense on the Danish island of Funen, the washerwoman wife of a poor cobbler gave birth to a son. The year was 1805 and the infant, Hans Christian Andersen, grew up to become the most famous Dane who has ever lived. His fairytales and other writings have been translated into more than 100 languages.

Andersen's talents surfaced at an early age: he painted, sang, danced and acted. His father died when he was 11 and he was left in the care of his

paternal grandmother. Three years later he set off for Copenhagen to seek his fortune, dreaming of fame as an actor or ballet dancer.

But Andersen's life was dogged by disappointment and sadness, all of which is recorded in his personal diaries and his autobiography, *The Story of My Life* (1847). Although he attended the Royal Theatre School, he never achieved more than a walk-on part as a troll. It was made clear to him that his ambitions on the ballet stage would be thwarted by his physical appearance – his nose was large and he was generally considered ugly. He felt lonely and unloved, suffering particularly from an unrequited passion for the Swedish singer, Jenny Lind.

And yet, it was his unhappiness and loneliness that gave rise to his extraordinary creativity as a writer of fairy stories. The poignancy of *The Ugly Duckling*, for example, comes straight from the heart. The Chinese emperor's yearning for *The Nightingale* is his own for Jenny Lind (whose nickname was 'the Swedish Nightingale'). Even so, his fairy stories all end happily, reflecting the fact that sadness never embittered him. Without his essential warmth and humanity, these and other immortal classics, such as *The Princess and the Pea* and *The Little Mermaid*, could not have touched the hearts and minds of countless millions of children and adults.

The fame and fortune he achieved appears not to have fulfilled him, nor did it assuage his sadness or still his restlessness. He mixed with the rich and famous, but lived in temporary accommodation, never putting down roots; he toured Europe 29 times before his death in 1875.

In 2005 the 200th anniversary of Andersen's birth was celebrated all over Denmark with numerous festivities, exhibitions and events.

Facing page: Copenhagen's tribute to the weaver of magical tales
Above: 'Hans Christian Andersen' and his characters parade along the Odense riverbank; below: the little house in Odense where Andersen was born

A spectacular view that sweeps all the way down to the distant horizon from Svendborg

Svendborg

Svendborg is Funen's second-largest city, and the gateway to Tåsinge, Langeland, Ærø and the Funen archipelago's smaller southern islands. Svendborg is more charming than Odense and has commanding views out over the islands and along the south Funen coast. Steep, narrow and winding streets lead down to the sheltered harbour, which was once the Hanseatic trading port on which Svendborg's prosperity was built and is now a major yachting marina. It is also the start and finishing point of the **Fyn Rundt wooden ships race**, held each July.

The Svendborgsund bridge that spans more than 1km (⅔ mile) of water links the island of Tåsinge to the city.

Svendborg is 24km (15 miles) east of Fåborg.

Tåsinge

For many people Tåsinge island is no more than a staging post on the way from Funen to Langeland, but a stop here is rewarding. Those who turn off the main road at the end of the bridge from Svendborg find that the atmosphere changes suddenly to one of gentle seclusion. This is a very green and gently undulating agricultural island, sprinkled with orchards, ponds and thatched farmhouses. Its gem is the immaculately preserved little village of **Troense**, with half-timbered waterfront houses looking over a yacht harbour and across the narrow stretch of water to tiny Thurø. Valdemars Castle is located just outside the village.

Tåsinge lies south of Funen, 1km (⅔ mile) south of the port of Svendborg.

Valdemars Slot (Valdemar's Castle)
Like many Danish castles, this is really
more of a stately mansion. It was built
by Christian IV between 1639 and 1644
for his son, Count Valdemar Christian,
who died in battle soon afterwards.
Naval hero Niels Juel was awarded the
castle in 1678 for his exploits in the
wars against Sweden. He added the
sumptuous baroque-style royal
apartment and halls. The vast kitchen
and candlelit chapel are also worth
seeing. Even if the museum is closed,
the grounds are still worth a visit;
wander up from the sandy beach just
a short distance away, and gaze at the
imposing façade across the beautiful
ornamental lake.
*Valdemars Slot Herregårdsmuseum:
Slotsalleen 100, 1km (⅔ mile) east of
Troense. Tel: 62 22 61 06;
www.valdemarsslot.dk. Open: from
Easter, daily 10am–5pm;
Apr, weekends 10am–5pm; May–Sept,
daily 10am–5pm (closed on Mon in Sept);
Oct, daily 10am–5pm. Admission charge.*

Valdemar's Castle, dating from the 17th century

Walk: Odense

This gentle amble takes in the pedestrianised heart of Odense, passing through gardens and along the river, and giving you a feel of a city that reflects the peace and gentleness of Funen island of which it is the capital. (*For map, see p75.*)

Allow 2 hours.

The walk starts outside the railway station, where the Railway Museum is worth exploring.

1 Jernbanemuseet (Railway Museum)

The museum covers the history of Danish railways, illustrated by real and model locomotives and carriages dating back 150 years.

Leave the museum via the railway station and follow Jernbanegade southwards, passing the Fyns Kunstmuseum (Funen Art Gallery) on the left at No 13.

Modern sculpture adds a touch of the whimsical at Odense, world capital of the fairytale

Turn left at the end of the road, following Vestergade into Flakhaven.

2 Flakhaven

Flakhaven marks the heart of the historic red-brick city centre. The statue of Frederik VII is juxtaposed with a rather bizarre abstract sculpture. Dominating the square is the imperious 57-m (187-ft) long façade of the 1883 Rådhuset, in a jumble of architectural styles. Visit the interior to see a variety of paintings by Funen artists, including Johannes Larsen. The tourist office is also inside.

Cross to the south of the square and enter the cathedral (see p77), which is frequently empty of visitors, despite being one of the finest in Denmark.

3 Sankt Knuds Domkirke (Saint Canute's Cathedral)

One of the cathedral's secret treats is to creep into the crypt, following in the footsteps of millions of earlier pilgrims whose feet have worn down the stone stairs that lead to the tombs of Saints Canute and Alban (Sankt Albani).

Follow a path from the cathedral down to the grassy bank of the Odense Å (Odense River) and cross a wooden footbridge on to the HC Andersen Haven (gardens) on

an island. *Note the metal sculptures of Andersen's fairytale characters which appear to be floating on the calm lake. Follow the path round the island and leave it via the third footbridge leading into Klosterbakken. Take the first turning on the right for Munkemøllestræde. The tiny house at Nos 3–5 is where Andersen lived from the age of two until his departure for Copenhagen at 14.*

4 HC Andersen's Barndomshjem (House)

The author described this house as having 'One single room where all the space was taken up by the workshop, the bed and the bench where I slept'. The house in fact has two rooms; the other was occupied by another family.

Leaving the house turn right, cutting through to Klaregade, which leads over the river. On the other side turn immediately right on to a footpath through the gardens.

5 Munkemose (Gardens)

Finish the walk by wandering through this expanse of greenery and herbaceous borders, looking across the River Odense with its overhanging willows, anglers and flotillas of ducks.

Railway Museum
24 Dannebrogsgade. Tel: 66 13 66 30. Open: May–Sept, daily 10am–4pm; Oct–Apr, Tue–Sun 10am–1pm, closed: Mon. Admission charge.
Rådhuset
Flakhaven. Tel: 66 13 13 72. Open: Mon–Wed 9am–3.30pm, Thur 9am–5.30pm, Fri 9am–noon. Closed: Sat & Sun. Admission charge.
HC Andersen's House
Tel: 65 51 46 01. Open: daily, June–Sept 10am–5pm; Oct–May 11am–3pm. Admission charge.

Picturesque old Odense

By bike: south Funen

This ride passes through some of Funen's most enchanting landscapes, exploring small villages, hidden lanes and historic houses. The steeper gradients require effort, and there are many opportunities for short walking detours. *Allow 3 hours.*

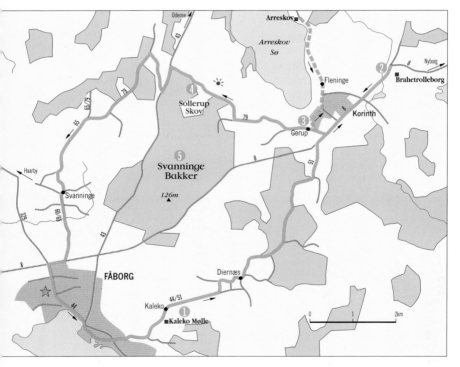

Starting in Fåborg, hire a bicycle from Bjarnes Cykler on Svendborgvej 69 and set off eastwards along the waterfront road, turning left on to the signposted cycle Route 51 (Road No 44). After about 2km (1¼ miles) of gentle uphill cycling, a mill comes into view on the right.

1 Kaleko Mølle

This is the oldest working watermill in Denmark, parts of it dating to the 17th century. Inside is a small museum arranged with old furniture and objects illustrating the home and working life of a miller and his family in the 19th century. Next to the mill is the stream and millpond, an old barn and a stable, all set amid fields and with woodland beyond. *Continue up Route 51, through Korinth. On the right-hand side of the straight road just beyond the village, look for a large manor house with a church and spire alongside.*

Bicycle paths line most of the roads in Denmark

2 Brahetrolleborg
Originally a Cistercian monastery from 1172, parts of this large manor house complex, including the church and outbuildings, date from the 13th century. Further remains of the monastery were discovered during restoration work in 1985. The park is open to the public.
Return the short distance to Korinth and turn right (westwards) on to Cycle Route 79 – a leafy lane that meanders into the hills. After about 1km (²/₃ mile), you reach Gerup.

3 Gerup
The old school building, built in 1784, is one of the oldest in Denmark. It has been turned into a small school museum illustrating the changing life of teachers and pupils at rural schools from the 18th to the 20th centuries.

From here, if you have time, it is worth turning right to detour beside the narrow lake as far as Arreskov manor house on the left, before returning to Route 79.
Continue for about another 2km (1¼ miles) to the Sollerup picnic spot on the right.

4 Sollerup Skov (Sollerup Woods)
There are beautiful views over Arreskov Sø, Funen's largest lake, and the undulating hills and forest beyond.

Continue along Cycle Route 79, bearing left at its junction with Cycle Route 65 (Road No 43) turning south. Soon the high spire of Svanninge's church comes into view.

5 Svanninge Bakker (Nature Park)
In typically Danish self-deprecating fashion, these gentle, wooded hills of winding lanes and country houses are often called the 'Funen Alps'. At the farm 'Kastanjely', in Svanninge village, information is available on footpaths and nature trails in the Svanninge Bakker (Nature Park), as well as explanations of the flora, fauna and geology. The highest point is 126m (413ft) above sea level. At the top of one 85-m (279-ft) hill is a tower that can be climbed, free of charge, for a 360-degree panorama.
From Svanninge continue gently downhill on Cycle Route 60, then Cycle Route 65 to Road No 8. Turn right, then immediately left on to Road No 44, which will take you back to Fåborg.

Kaleko Mølle
Prices Havevej, Diernæs.
Tel: 62 61 33 38; www.fkm.nu.
Open: June–Sept, daily 10.30am–4.30pm.
Admission charge.
Brahetrolleborg
Reventlowsvej 1, Korinth, Fåborg.
Tel: 61 65 10 04. Open: mid-Apr–mid-Oct, daily 8am–4pm. Admission charge.

Jutland (Jylland)

Jutland is Denmark's 'finger', the northward-pointing peninsula that accounts for around 70 per cent of the country's land area, though only about 45 per cent of its population. Since Viking times, Denmark's power has been focused eastwards on Zealand, allowing Jutland to retain the calmness of its people and peacefulness of its countryside.

North Sea ferries land at Esbjerg, also Scandinavia's largest fishing port

Between the German border and the tip of Jutland (about 400km/249 miles to the north) the peninsula divides into three distinct geographical areas, each differing markedly in scenery and atmosphere. South Jutland is flat and marshy, with large herds of cattle grazing

A typical Jutland thatched cottage

fertile pastures. Modern wind farms contrast strikingly with ancient market towns, such as Ribe and Tønder. The region's history is entwined with that of its neighbour, Germany. **South Jutland**, then called North Sleswig, was captured by Prussia in 1864, and returned to Denmark in 1920 after a plebiscite.

Denmark at its gentlest is found in **Mid-Jutland**. The countryside of the so-called 'Lake District' is rippled with hills and sprinkled with lakes, forests and streams; on the east coast, villages huddle round safe harbours. Everything appears to be on a miniature scale, as if a parody of Danish understatement.

The Limfjord slices right through Jutland, from the North Sea to the Baltic. Beyond the fjord, the landscape of **Northern Jutland** becomes more rugged; the cosy atmosphere is discarded for something wilder, more exposed and closer to nature in the raw. There are superb beaches, great bald sand dunes and splintering inlets, redolent of Norway. At Skagen, on the peninsula's northern extremity, there is a sense of continuous climax where the two seas meet.

Jutland

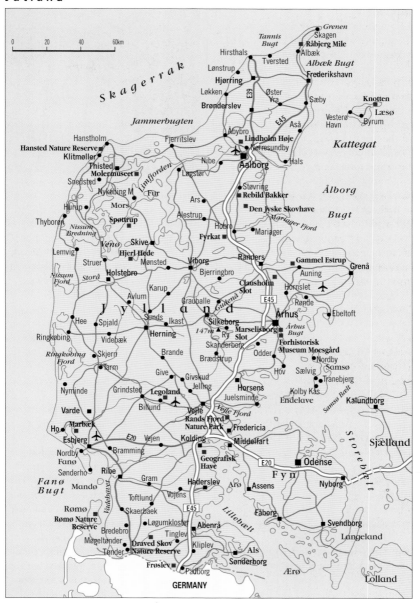

Grenen
Skagen
Tannis Bugt   Råbjerg Mile
Hirsthals   Albæk
Tversted   Albæk Bugt
Lønstrup   Frederikshavn
Hjørring
Løkken   Øster   Sæby   Knotten
Brønderslev   Vrå   Vesterø   Læsø
Havn   Byrum
Aså
Jammerbugten   Åbybro
Hanstholm   Fjerritslev   Lindholm Høje   Kattegat
Hansted Nature Reserve   Nørresundby
Klitmøller   Nibe   Aalborg   Hals
Thisted
Molermuseet   Løgstør
Snedsted   Ålborg
Nykøbing M   Fur   Støvring   Bugt
Hurup   Mors   Rebild Bakker
Thyborøn   Ars   Den Jyske Skovhave
Nissum   Alestrup   Mariager Fjord
Bredning   Spøttrup   Hobro
Skive   Fyrkat   Mariager
Lemvig   Hjerl Hede
Struer   Mønsted   Viborg   Randers
Nissum   Storå   Holstebro   Bjerringbro   Gammel Estrup
Fjord   Auning   Grenå
Karup   Clausholm   Hornslet
Avlum   Slot   Rønde
Jylland   Grauballe   E45
Hee   Spjald   Sunds   Ikast   Silkeborg   Århus
Ringkøbing   Videbæk   Herning   147m   Ry   Marselisborg   Ebeltoft
Slot   Århus
Ringkøbing   Brande   Skanderborg   Bugt
Fjord   Skjern   Forhistorisk
Tarm   Give   Odder   Museum Moesgård
Nyminde   Givskud   Nordby
Grindsted   Jelling   Hov   Sælvig   Samsø
Varde   Legoland   Horsens   Tranebjerg
Billund   Juelsminde   Kolby Kås
Ho   Marbæk   Vejle   Endelave   Kalundborg
Rands Fjord   Vejle Fjord
Esbjerg   Nature Park   Fredericia   Storebælt
Nordby   E20   Vejen   Kolding   Middelfart   Sjælland
Fanø   Bramming
Sønderho   Ribe   Geografisk   E20   Odense
Fanø   Mandø   Gram   Have   Fyn
Bugt   Haderslev   Årø   Assens   Nyborg
Toftlund   Vojens
Rømø   Skaerbæk   Fåborg
Rømø Nature   Løgumkloster   Åbenrå   Svendborg
Reserve   Bredebro   Tinglev   Langeland
Møgeltønder   Draved Skov   Kliplev   Als
Tønder   Nature Reserve   Lolland
Frøslev   Sønderborg   Ærø
Padborg

GERMANY

Skagerrak

0   20   40   60km

E39
E5
E45
E20
E45

GERMANY

Aalborg

Throughout Scandinavia the name of Denmark's fourth-largest city is linked with Aquavit, the popular grain spirit, flavoured with caraway seeds, that is distilled here. Natives of the city, however, appear to be more intoxicated on their rich history and heritage. Their pride in all things traditional is reflected in the fact that when, in 1948, the Danish double A was changed to Å (as in Århus, for example), the city refused to comply. So Aalborg it is, although the sacrilegious Ålborg is sometimes used.

St Botolph's, a 15th-century cathedral at the heart of a modern city

Aalborg was founded in Viking times, at the narrowest point on the Limfjord, its strategic location making it an important transport junction for trade with Norway and Sweden. Today the city is an important industrial centre.
109km (68 miles) north of Århus. Tourist office: Østerågade 8. Tel: 99 30 60 90; www.visitaalborg.com

Aalborg Historiske Museum (Historical Museum)

This museum is worth visiting for the 1602 Aalborg Room – a chamber of woodcarved panelling and coffered ceilings all taken from a wealthy merchant's house and painstakingly reassembled. Other displays span the city's history from the Stone Age through to the present.
Algade 48. Tel: 99 31 74 00; www.aahm.dk. Open: Tue–Sun 10am–5pm. Closed: Mon. Admission charge.

Aalborg Sofarts-og Marinemuseum (Aalborg Maritime Museum)

Climb aboard the *Springeren*, a real submarine over 50m (164ft) long, and wander its claustrophobic corridors and conning tower. There are several other retired naval vessels in this shipyard on the Limfjord, as well as an excellent oceanography section where you can measure the current and water temperature in the fjord.
Vestre Fjordvej 81. Tel: 98 11 78 03. Open: Sept–Apr, daily 10am–4pm; May–Aug 10am–6pm. Admission charge.

Budolfi Domkirke (St Botolph's Cathedral)

The carillon that plays every hour (from 9am to 10pm) will indicate in which direction to head. Most of the whitewashed brick church was built around 1400, although some remnants survive of a church 300 years older. The baroque spire was added in 1779. Inside, the vast altarpiece, the marble font and the fine carved pulpit are worth a look, but the real treasures of this cathedral are the superb frescoes. The entrance porch is itself a former chapel adorned with pictorial representations of Abraham's sacrifice of Isaac and the touching

legend of the fig tree that bowed down to the infant Jesus on the flight to Egypt. On the south wall are some wonderfully colourful frescoes of centaurs and the life of St Catherine of Alexandria.
Algade. Tel: 98 12 46 70.
Open: Oct–Apr, Mon–Fri 9am–3pm, Sat until noon; May–Sept, Mon–Fri 9am–4pm, Sat until noon. Free admission.

Jens Bangs Stenhus (Jens Bang's House)
This grand five-storey mansion of 1624 is the largest Renaissance building in Scandinavia. Bang was a wealthy merchant who surrounded himself with splendour, but it is the eccentricities reflecting his personality that attract

most attention. Argumentative and obstinate, he made many enemies and caricatured them in the shape of the grotesque gargoyles that can been seen on the façade. The face looking out on the south side, rudely sticking out its tongue at the Rådhuset, is said to represent Bang who is expressing his disgust at his failure to be elected to the town council.

The building is still a pharmacy, as it has been for more than 300 years. The vaulted basement was a secret meeting place for the Danish Resistance during World War II. It is now a popular wine bar, full of atmosphere.
Østerågade 9, next to the tourist office.

Aalborg town plan

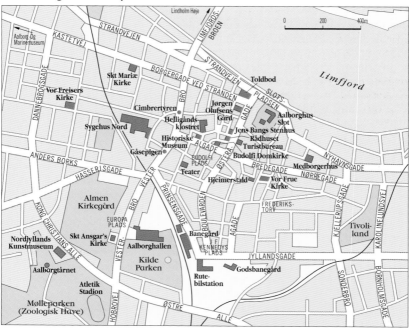

Lindholm Høje: there was no greater honour for a Viking warrior than to die in battle

Nordjyllands Kunstmuseum (North Jutland Arts Museum)

The white marble and glass exterior of this ultra-modern building, located at the edge of an expansive wooded park, is perfectly suited to what it contains – the most important collections of modern art in Denmark. Natural light streams into the galleries where the exhibits can be viewed in their extravagant, wide-open display areas. Contemporary Danish artists predominate, but there are also works by Andy Warhol and Max Ernst. Youngsters can discard inhibitions in the children's section, where they can touch exhibits and make as much noise as they want.

Outside, the sculpture park is dominated by Bjørn Nørgaard's acclaimed **Dream Palace**, a pyramid made of glass. An amphitheatre hosts open-air plays and concerts, normally held in summer.

Kong Christians Allé 50. Tel: 98 13 80 88;
www.nordjyllandskunstmuseum.dk.
Open: Tue–Sun 10am–5pm. Closed: Mon.
Admission charge.

Nearby
Lindholm Høje

This Iron Age and Viking settlement and burial ground is one of the most important archaeological sites in Denmark. Nearly 700 graves have been excavated and the finds are displayed in the museum to the west of the site. The museum also has a series of tableaux illustrating life in the village.

These remains were found, perfectly preserved, in 1952, having been buried by drifting sand in about AD 1000.
Lindholm Høje is at Nørresundby, which lies north of the Limfjord, directly opposite Aalborg to which it is connected by a bridge and tunnel. From Aalborg take bus No 6 (Uttrup Nord).
Vendilavej 11, 9400 Nørresundby.
Tel: 99 31 74 40;

are several reconditioned and refitted fishing boats from different eras that can be entered and explored, as well as some rebuilt fishermen's houses.

The museum also has an aquarium and sealarium. Instead of the selection of exotic specimens common to most aquariums, this one is largely devoted to the Atlantic and Baltic fish on which the industry depends. Seals can be watched underwater through the glass wall of their tank. Children will find feeding times particularly exciting.
Saltvandsakvariet, Tarphagevej 2–6. Tel: 76 12 20 00; www.fimus.dk. Open: daily, Sept–June 10am–5pm; July & Aug 10am–6pm. Admission charge.

Esbjerg Museum
The city's main museum houses two separate exhibitions, both of which are worth a visit, even a short one.

The first demonstrates life in the city between 1890 and 1940 with some authentic tableaux, and explains how the fishing and mercantile port burgeoned into a major city. The second, more recent, exhibition is of earlier life in the area and on nearby Fanø (*see p96*).

Another small museum of amber is also housed here.
Torvegade 45. Tel: 75 12 78 11; www.esbjergmuseum.dk. Open: daily 10am–4pm. Closed: Sept–May on Mon. Admission charge.

Inside Esbjerg's Fisheries and Maritime Museum

Fanø

Just 20 minutes by ferry across a narrow strip of water from Esbjerg, Fanø is the city's playground. The island is 18km (11 miles) long and its forested interior is crisscrossed by footpaths and cycling trails. In summer the main attraction is the long sandy beach on the west coast, where many families have holiday homes. There are also several campsites.

The main village is **Nordby**, where there are two good museums. The **Fanø Museum** charts the evolving lifestyle of the Fanø islanders and has a collection of oddities from around the world, brought back by sailors. The **Fanø Søfarts-og Dragtudstilling Museum** (Maritime and Costume Museum) displays model ships and local dress from throughout the ages. Quaint little thatched and half-timbered houses make **Sønderho** village, to the south, worth visiting.

Tourist office: Havnepladsen, Nordby. Tel: 75 16 26 00.
Maritime and Costume Museum: Tel: 75 16 22 72. Open: May–Sept, Mon–Sat 10am–5pm.
The Fanø ferry (tel: 76 11 54 50) takes 20 minutes and leaves from Esbjerg harbour every half hour from May–Sept, and every hour from Oct–Apr.

Fjerritslev

Fjerritslev is the principal tourist town of Han Herred – the land between the Limfjorden and the sea. With several hotels and a scattering of holiday homes, it makes an excellent base for exploring the beaches and countryside of North Jutland. The town is also home to the **Fjerritslev Bryggeri-og Egnsmuseum** (Fjerritslev Brewing Museum), next to the tourist office. The museum is housed in the Kjeldgaard brewery which closed in 1968 but has

Frederikshavn has a truly Scandinavian air about it, being as much Norwegian and Swedish as Danish

been preserved intact, its brass still gleamingly polished.

Immediately north of Fjerritslev there are more than 30km (19 miles) of fine sandy beach. From Road No 11, tracks lead through the dunes to the popular swimming areas of **Tranum Strand**, **Torup Strand** and **Bulbjerg**.

Fjerritslev is 120km (75 miles) northwest of Århus, and 40km (25 miles) west of Aalborg.
Tourist office: Vestergade 16.
Tel: 98 21 16 55.

Frederikshavn

Frederikshavn is one of North Jutland's main ports, with ferry connections to various Norwegian and Swedish cities (including Oslo and Gothenburg) and to the remote island of Læsø (*see p140*). Around the fishing harbour is a small district of narrow streets and cottages, mostly painted yellow. There is also a much larger shopping district of pedestrianised precincts, where hordes of visitors from around Scandinavia come to shop for bargains in food, clothes and drink.

Just outside the town is the **Bangsbo** manor house and deer park.
60km (37 miles) northeast of Aalborg.
Tourist office: Skandiatorvet 1.
Tel: 98 42 32 66.

Frøslev

In 1944 the occupying Germans established a concentration camp at Frøslev, where some 13,000 Danes were held. Although the sort of atrocities perpetrated by the Nazis elsewhere did not happen here, some Danes suffered greatly when they were deported to

Memorial at Frøslev's former German concentration camp

other concentration camps in Germany. After the war, Danish collaborators were held here awaiting trial.

Some of the blocks at Frøslev have been preserved with their tight-packed bunk accommodation. The original main watchtower still looms intimidatingly. Other blocks house three small museums (with separate entrance charges). One illustrates the work of the Danish Red Cross Organisation from World War II until the present; the second demonstrates the work of Danish troops serving with the United Nations, including a force currently in Bosnia; the third, an exhibition mounted by Amnesty International, illustrates the extent of human rights violations around the world.

Danish/German frontier, 60km (37 miles) south of Kolding.
Museet for Froeslevlejren: Lejrvejen 83, Padborg. Tel: 74 67 65 57.
Open: Oct–Mar, Tue–Fri 9am–4pm, Sat & Sun 10am–5pm; Apr–Sept, daily 10am–5pm. Admission charge.

Gammel Estrup

The 16th-century Renaissance moated manor house castle of Gammel Estrup was for generations the home of two noble families – first the Broks and latterly the Scheels – both close advisors to the Crown. After the death of Count Scheel in 1936, his heirs sold the castle and contents, but two years later it was bought by his son-in-law, Valdemar Uttental, and the **Jyllands Herregårdsmuseum** (Jutland Manor House Museum) was established here. Many of the original furnishings and works of art have been re-acquired and are displayed in a sequence of styles, changing from room to room, following the character of each generation that lived in the castle.

The **Dansk Landbrugsmuseum** (Danish Agricultural Museum) is housed in a separate building within the castle grounds. Thousands of agricultural implements are displayed, with exhibitions explaining the evolution of farming over the last two centuries. There are changing exhibitions of paintings on agricultural themes, sculpture, ceramics and textiles. *Gammel Estrup is in the village of Auning, 38km (24 miles) north of Århus. Jyllands Herregårdsmuseum tel: 86 48 30 01. Open: Jan–Mar, Nov & Dec, Tue–Sun 10am–3pm; Apr–June, Sept & Oct, daily 10am–5pm; July & Aug, daily 10am–6pm. Admission charge.*

Hobro

Strategically positioned at the head of the Mariager Fjord (*see p106*), Hobro was founded as a Viking settlement in AD 980 and is a good base for exploring the region. Archaeological finds from Fyrkat (*see opposite*) are housed in the **Sydhimmerlands Museum**, as well as collections of glass, porcelain and silver. *46km (29 miles) south of Aalborg. Tourist office: Store Torv. Tel: 96 57 66 13.*

Like most aristocratic homes in Denmark, Gammel Estrup now houses a museum

Sydhimmerlands Museum:
Vestergade 23. Tel: 98 51 05 55;
www.sydhimmerlandsmuseum.dk.
Open: Mar & Apr, weekends 11am–4pm;
May–Sept, daily 11am–4pm; on the first
two weekends in Oct & the 42nd week of
the year 11am–4pm. Admission charge.

Nearby
Fyrkat
One of only four known Viking forts in
Denmark, Fyrkat was believed to have
been built as a military base, on the
orders of Harald Bluetooth, in around
AD 980. The smallest of the four, Fyrkat
was constructed of wooden staves with a
precision and strict symmetry rare
anywhere in the Viking world. It has
been rebuilt with equal attention to
detail, with circular ramparts enclosing
three rooms which once would have
housed about 50 people.

A reproduction Viking house outside
the fort, and a Viking farm about 500m
(1,640ft) away, demonstrate life in the
10th century, based on knowledge
gained from excavating the site.
3km (2 miles) west of Hobro.
Vikingecenter Fyrkat, Fyrkatvej 37B.
Tel: 98 51 19 27; www.fyrkat.dk.
Open: Mar–May, Sept & Oct 10am–4pm;
June–Aug 10am–5pm. Admission charge.

Holstebro
Five major roads converge at this market
town on the River Storå, which staged
one of Denmark's greatest medieval ox
fairs. A series of major fires destroyed
the historic heart of the town, although
the 1907 church does contain several
treasures rescued from its incinerated
predecessor, including a superb

Archaeological work at Fyrkat has provided vital
insights into Viking life

16th-century Dutch altarpiece and a
48-bell carillon.

Holstebro has compensated for its loss
with two excellent art galleries. The
Holstebro Art Museum exhibits a large
and varied collection of contemporary
Danish work, plus ethnic art from Bali,
Peru, Tibet and various parts of Africa.
The **Jens Nielsen and Olivia Holm-
Møller Collection** is composed largely
of the works of these two artists,
supplemented with works by other
Danish artists.
52km (32 miles) west of Viborg. Tourist
office: Den Røde Plads 14. Tel: 97 42 57 00.
Holstebro Kunstmuseum: Museumsvej 2.
Tel: 97 42 45 18. Open: Sept–June,
Tue–Fri noon–4pm, Sat & Sun
11am–5pm; July–Aug, Tue–Sun
11am–5pm. Admission charge.
Jens Nielsen and Olivia Holm-Møller
Collection: Nørrebrogade 1. Tel: 97 42 18
24. Open: Tue–Fri noon–4pm, Sat & Sun
11am–5pm. Admission charge.

Some visitors to Denmark expect to encounter vast herds of swine snuffling and grunting their way through the countryside. So renowned has Danish bacon become that, along with pastries and blue cheese, the country and product are automatically associated in millions of minds across Europe and further afield.

In fact, you could easily drive from one end of Denmark to the other without ever glimpsing a pink snout or curly tail. Nor, in a score of lavish breakfast buffets, would you necessarily so much as sniff at a rasher of streaky bacon. Danish pigs are intensively farmed, often indoors, and the canny Danes export almost all of the meat. Not only does Danish bacon grace millions of British, Dutch and German breakfast tables, huge quantities of fresh pork constitute Denmark's single most lucrative export to Japan. On the basis of this, Denmark is the only European Union country to enjoy a trade surplus with Japan.

In truth, the ultra-efficient farming of pigs is only one facet of the sweeping revolution which has calmly taken place under the gentle, placid exterior of the Danish countryside. In 1950 there were around 200,000 farms employing 20 per cent of the population. Today, there are about 67,000 farms, with agriculture employing just 4 per cent of the population. The average size of a farm is about 40ha (99 acres), and most holdings are worked almost exclusively by the families that own them. Almost

two-thirds of the country is used for farming. Sixty per cent of the country's agricultural production is cereals, and 20 per cent is used as grazing pasture; most of the remainder is used either for rearing pigs and other livestock, or for growing beet, though there is still a strong fur industry in Denmark.

Strict rationalisation of farming has led Denmark to produce a limited range of produce, but of excellent quality. So efficient is this industry that Denmark actually produces enough to feed 15 million people – three times its population.

Bucolic scenes of the Danish countryside; however, much of the farming is intensive

A tower is required to lend 'Sky Mountain', Denmark's highest point, a hint of credibility

Horsens

This commercial and industrial town, at the head of the broad Horsens Fjord, dates from the 12th century. First impressions, however, are of a more modern town, especially along Søndergade, the wide, pedestrianised main shopping street. There you will see the grand façade of the **Jørgensen Hotel**, the former Lichtenberg Palace, built for a rich merchant in 1744.

For a more intimate sense of Horsens, turn down any of the narrow traffic-free side streets leading off the Søndergade. The main square in the town centre is dedicated to Horsens' most famous son, the explorer and cartographer Vitus Bering (1680–1741), after whom the Bering Sea and Strait are named.

The small town has several museums, and the one not to be missed is the **Industrimuseet** (Museum of Industry), which has some wonderful old industrial machinery, gleamingly restored.

40km (25 miles) southwest of Århus.
Tourist office: Søndergade 26.
Tel: 75 60 21 20.
Industrimuseet: Gasvej 17–19. Tel: 75 60 07 88; www.industrimuseet.dk.
Open: July & Aug, daily 10am–4pm; Sept–June, Tue–Sun 11am–4pm.
Admission charge.

Kolding

Founded in the 13th century, Kolding is one of the most important junction towns in East Jutland, with roads converging upon it from all parts of the peninsula. The town is dominated by the massive **Koldinghus Castle**, originally built by King Erik V in 1268 but almost entirely rebuilt by various later monarchs. The earliest preserved sections are of the 15th century. In the 18th century it fell into disrepair. A lengthy period of rebuilding started in 1890 to create the museum which today contains an awesome collection of Romanesque and Gothic church sculpture, furniture, early Danish painting, ceramics and silver. From the top of the Giants' Tower there are superb views over the town.
70km (43 miles) southwest of Århus.
Tourist office: Akseltorv 8.
Tel: 76 33 21 00.
Museet på Koldinghus tel: 76 33 81 00; www.koldinghus.dk. Open: daily 10am–5pm. Admission charge.

Lake District

In many ways, Denmark's Lake District reflects the character of the country as a whole – undramatic, understated, yet with an exceptionally rich history and a calm, peaceful allure. This is a region of placid lakes, serpentine rivers and forested hills lying to the west of Århus in west Jutland. At the heart of the region is **Himmelbjerget** (literally the '**Sky Mountain**'), the highest point in Denmark at just 147m (482ft) above sea level. It can be reached by road from the nearby town of **Ry**, which is the regional centre for such outdoor activities as cycling, canoeing and hiking.

From the top of Himmelbjerget, there are panoramic views over the hills and lakes. A winding path leads down from the summit to a jetty on the long, narrow **Lake Julsø**, where MS *Hjejlen*, claimed to be the world's oldest working paddle steamer, calls on its summer lake cruises from Silkeborg, the Lake District's main town.

Though modern and comparatively featureless, **Silkeborg** is worth visiting for its museum, where '**Tollund Man**' (*see p119*) is the principal exhibit.
Silkeborg is 40km (25 miles) west of Århus. Tourist office: Åhavevej 2A.
Tel: 86 82 19 11.
Silkeborg Kulturhistoriske Museum:
Hovedgaardsen, Hovedgaardsvej 7.
Tel: 86 82 14 99;
www.silkeborgmuseum.dk.
Open: May–mid-Oct, daily 10am–5pm;
mid-Oct–Apr, Wed, Sat & Sun
noon–4pm. Admission charge.

Parts of Koldinghus Castle go back to the 15th century

Denmark's top tourist attraction – meticulously constructed from miniature bricks

when they grow up the ultimate dream job. However, only a handful are fortunate enough to get jobs building the features at Legoland – the theme park created with some 50 million Lego bricks. With more than a million visitors a year, Legoland is Denmark's leading tourist attraction. One of the most popular features is X-treme Racers, a 400-m (1,312-ft) roller coaster which reaches speeds of up to 60km/h (37mph). This is the most extreme ride at Legoland Billund and is a large-scale replica of the popular Lego Racers. At

Legoland

The story of Legoland started with an unemployed Danish carpenter in the 1930s. He began to make wooden toys which he called Lego from the Danish words *leg godt*, meaning 'play well'. In 1947 he opened his first factory making plastic bricks. In 1968, with Lego by now a global phenomenon, Legoland Park opened at Billund.

There are roughly 360 million Lego engineers around the world. Most of them would consider playing with the world-famous coloured bricks for real

Pirateland visitors can join Captain Roger in his secret cave for feasts and treasure hunts. The miniature train, leading into a mountain cavern full of gold diggers, and a Lego safari, where a zebra-striped jeep takes you through a savanna of life-sized elephants, giraffes, crocodiles and other wild animals, are also very popular.

Throughout the tourist season the park also hosts numerous events, from theme days focusing on Legoland's gardens and teddy bear days, to song contests, dressing up days and pop concerts. One recent innovation is a Legoland After Dark weekend with torchlight, night-time parades and fireworks displays.

At the Lego traffic school, children between 8 and 13 years are given a 20-minute course in road safety as they learn to drive Lego cars, completing a course for which Legoland driving licences are issued. For younger children there are also Duplo (the larger-scale version of Lego) car and aeroplane rides. A monorail encircles the entire park and small electric self-drive boats carry their passengers down the Nile to Abu Simbel in Egypt, then to a Japanese emperor's palace, by way of the Athenian Acropolis and New York's Statue of Liberty.

The attention to detail is amazing,

particularly in the remarkable reproductions of Copenhagen's Amalienborg Castle, Amsterdam's Canal Circle, Austria's Tyrol region and 'Medbourne', a fictitious English town that combines elements from Stamford, Chester and York.

In the Indoor Collection there are swimming-pool-sized pits of Lego and Duplo to play with, Titania's Palace, a vast (non-Lego) palace with more than 3,000 miniature pieces in 18 rooms, and a huge collection of antique toys.

Legoland is 10 minutes' walk from the arrivals terminal at Billund airport. Legoland Park: Billund. Tel: 75 33 13 33; www.legoland.dk. Open: Apr–end-Oct daily at 10am; closing times vary. Admission charge.

Legoland's toy helicopters are large enough for children to climb into

A night watchman in Ribe

Mariager Fjord

Denmark's longest fjord snakes into the eastern side of Jutland between Århus and Aalborg. Lined by wooded slopes and meadows that sweep down to the water's edge, this is an area popular with cyclists, walkers, sailors and windsurfers.

Enchanting Mariager village, on the south bank of the fjord, is worth visiting simply to wander the cobbled streets of yellow, half-timbered cottages leading down to the marina. There is a small museum displaying local archaeological finds and exhibits explaining 18th-century life in the town. Little remains of 15th-century Mariager Abbey, though some beautiful frescoes survive in the church.

Mariager is 45km (28 miles) north of Århus. Tourist office: Torvet 1B. Tel: 98 54 13 77.

Mariager Museum: Kirkegade 4A. Tel: 98 54 12 87. Open: mid-May–mid-Sept 11am–5pm. Admission charge.

Randers

Denmark's sixth-largest city (with a population of around 56,000) straddles the River Gudenå in East Jutland. The modern industrial town has a thriving cultural life, and supports its own symphony orchestra. A modern concert hall and theatre have been constructed in a former power station known as the Værket.

Randers' history can be traced to the 11th century, when rebels opposing Saint Knut are recorded as having met here. In the Middle Ages this was a thriving trading port with access to the sea via the Gudenå. Many fine old houses survive in the central shopping areas around Brødregade, Storegade, Houmeden and Rådhusstræde.

Randers' Kulturhuset (Cultural Centre) contains the city's two main museums. The **Randers Kunstmuseum** (Randers Art Gallery) has an excellent collection of contemporary Danish art, including works by Lundstrøm, Søndergaard and Jorn. The **Kulturhistorisk Museum** (Cultural History Museum) traces the development of Danish culture from early drawings and artefacts through to 20th-century creations.

36km (22 miles) north of Århus.
Tourist office: Tørvebryggen 12.
Tel: 86 42 44 77; www.visitranders.com

Ribe

Rising out of the flat, marshy wetlands south of Esbjerg, and claimed as Denmark's oldest town, Ribe's history dates back to AD 800, when it was a Viking trading settlement. Before the Reformation (1536) there were no fewer than nine abbeys and 13 churches here, as well as many other Catholic institutions. Most were closed, and a combination of fires, floods and plague, plus the silting up of the River Å, further reduced the town's eminence.

Today, Ribe remains a small and beautifully preserved medieval town, with hundreds of half-timbered houses along its ancient cobbled streets

In contrast to its placid appearance today, Ribe was an important trading centre in the Middle Ages

Brave fishermen lost at sea are remembered at Skagen

30km (19 miles) southeast of Esbjerg.
Tourist office: Torvet 3–5.
Tel: 75 42 15 00; www.visitribe.dk.
Ribe Domkirke: Torvet. Tel: 75 42
06 19; www.ribe-domkirke.dk.
Open: Nov–Mar 11am–3pm; Apr & Oct
11am–4pm; May–Sept 10am–5pm.
Admission charge.

Ringkøbing

The old market town of Ringkøbing
stands on the northern shore of the
wide, calm Ringkøbing Fjord – the
lagoon that is linked to the North Sea by
a narrow neck of water at Nymindegab,
at its southern tip. Founded as a trading
port in the 13th century, Ringkøbing
remained an important seafaring town
until this channel silted up in the
18th century.

Access to the sea was severely limited
until 1931, when locks were built at
Hvide Sande, breaching the narrow spit
of land and reopening the fjord.

Even so, the fishing boats that land
their catch at Ringkøbing harbour
mainly operate in the fjord. A fish
auction takes place on Mondays,
Wednesdays and Fridays in the new red
wooden building at the edge of the
harbour, starting at 9.30am.

The **Ringkøbing Museum** (tel: 97 32
16 15) has a good collection of local
archaeological and historical finds, and
an excellent exhibition charting Mylius-
Erichsen's exploration of northeast
Greenland between 1906 and 1908.
Ringkøbing is 81km (50 miles) north of
Esbjerg.
Tourist office: Torvet.
Tel: 97 32 00 31;
www.ringkobing-tourist.dk

guaranteeing its popularity with
tourists. The sight not to be missed is
the cathedral, whose spire and tower are
visible from a long way off.

Construction work began in about
1150, with numerous subsequent
rebuildings and additions. Inside, grey
Romanesque arches contrast with the
bright white walls, and there are
monuments to various historical figures.
From the top of the 14th-century tower
there are expansive views over the
marshes and tidal flats.

Sæby

This delightfully quaint and peaceful fishing village, situated on Jutland's northeastern coast, was the site of a large 15th-century Carmelite monastery. A long and extraordinarily narrow church is all that survives of the monastery, which has a magnificent 16th-century Dutch altarpiece; how it reached Sæby remains a mystery. The walls are bedecked with striking murals, including one depicting the devil taking the soul of a dead man while his widow is being comforted by her lover.

45km (28 miles) northeast of Aalborg.
Tourist office: Krystaltorvet 1.
Tel: 98 46 12 44; www.saeby-tourist.dk

Skagen

Flung far out on the tip of Jutland's fingernail, Skagen is one of the treats of touring the Danish countryside. The Skagerrak and Kattegat seas – parts of the North Sea and the Baltic respectively – confront each other at this point in a perpetually churning commotion. The precise meeting point is at the end of a sand spit at **Grenen**, 3km (2 miles) north of the town, where the road finally peters out. You can walk out along the spit, and put a foot in each sea as gales blow from both directions. It is a rare instance of elemental drama in otherwise placid Denmark.

Tracks of a lone walker across the sand dunes at Råbjerg Mile, southwest of Skagen

Artists started settling in Skagen from the 1870s onwards, drawn by the rawness of the scenery and atmosphere, and by the startling clarity and brightness of its light. The **Brøndums Hotel** became their meeting place, and remains one of the main landmarks in this bohemian little town. Portraits of the various Skagen school artists, painted by one another, hang in the bar, the lounge and the dining room, and are a good introduction to their work.

The **Skagens Museum**, opposite the Brøndums Hotel, houses an excellent collection of their work in an airy setting that allows them to be viewed at their best. PS Krøyer, Laurits Tuxen and Michael and Anna Ancher (her father owned the Brøndums Hotel) are probably the best-known artists of the school. A canvas widely recognised as the finest ever to hail from the Skagen School is PS Krøyer's *Summer Evening on the South Beach at Skagen*. As well as landscapes that capture subtle changes of light at different times of the day, other popular subjects are fishermen dragging boats ashore and people walking on the beach at sunset.

Skagen is 102km (63 miles) north of Aalborg. Tourist office: Sankt Laurentii Vej 22. Tel: 98 44 13 77; www.skagen-tourist.dk. Skagens Museum: Brødumsvej 4. Tel: 98 44 64 44; www.skagensmuseum.dk. Open: June–Aug, daily 10am–6pm; May & Sept, daily 10am–5pm; Apr & Oct, Tue–Sun 11am–4pm; Nov–Mar, Wed–Fri 1–4pm, Sat 11am–4pm, Sun 11am–3pm. Admission charge.

Nearby

Nowhere else in Denmark is there anything quite like the wild, drifting sand dunes here, which are created by competing winds and sandstorms that rage across the northernmost tip of the country.

Signposted off Road 597 is the bald, Saharaesque **Råbjerg Mile**, located 12km (7 miles) southwest of Skagen and the highest of the dunes. It started advancing inland from the coast at Kandestederne beach a few centuries ago, and is expected to block Road 40, currently the only one to and from Skagen, within about 150 years.

Skive

This ancient little town on the Salling peninsula, now a busy tourist centre in summer, makes a good base for exploring the western end of the Limfjord (*see pp124–5*).

In the town itself, the **Skive Museum** is worth visiting for its extensive collection of locally found amber and pearls, as well as the **Vor Frue Kirke** (the Church of Our Lady) which has a particularly beautiful vaulted and frescoed ceiling.

Skive is 26km (16 miles) northwest of Viborg. Regional tourist office: Østerbro 7. Tel: 97 52 32 66; www.skive-egnen.dk

Sønderborg

Travellers crossing by ferry from south Jutland to south Fyn should stop at Sønderborg, near the German border, to visit one of the most important historical sites in Denmark, a battle site memorial with a singular atmosphere, unmatched anywhere else in the country.

Overlooking the town are the Dybbøl Banke military earthworks, a windmill, and a memorial stone to the hundreds of soldiers who died in the Prussian wars of 1848 and 1864. Denmark lost a third of Jutland in these defeats, which finally marked the end of the Danish empire that had once spread over much of Scandinavia. The memorial, set in a solemn and beautiful spot, is hauntingly evocative.

37km (23 miles) east of Padborg.

Tourist office: Rådhustorvet 7.
Tel: 74 42 35 55; www.visitals.dk

Tønder

This pretty little market town, in the southwestern corner of Denmark, near the German border, has a sleepy air, accentuated by the somnolent marshlands that stretch out to the

Vor Frue Kirke in Skive

north, south and west. The main pedestrianised shopping street (made up of Vestergade, Storegade and Østergade) is lined with well-preserved gabled houses, some bearing the coats of arms of wealthy 18th-century merchants.

Sixteenth-century **Kristkirken** (Christ Church) is worth seeing for its famous 17th-century rood screen. There are two museums: the **Tønder Museum** in the 16th-century tower gatehouse, which charts the town's history, including the story of its lacemaking industry; and the **Sønderjyllands Kunstmuseum** (South Jutland Art Museum) with its collection of 19th- and 20th-century Danish and German works.
Tønder is 44km (27 miles) west of Padborg. Tourist office: Torvet 1. Tel: 74 72 12 20; www.tdr-turist.dk

Vejle

Vejle is a busy commercial and industrial port town in East Jutland. It has a relaxed ambience, and is set in a beautiful region of gentle hills, forests, lakes, rivers and fjords.

The town, dating from the 12th century, rises fairly steeply from the harbour, with **Sankt Nikolai Kirke** (Saint Nicholas' Church) at the highest point. Inside the church is the body of an Iron Age woman, preserved in a peat bog and discovered in the 19th century (*see also pp118–19*).

A winding street leads up to a restored windmill, where there is a small exhibition of milling over the centuries. In the same building as the tourist office, which is in a former merchant's house, is a good local history museum. The **Vejle Kunstmuseum** (Vejle Art Museum) has a large collection of mainly Danish 20th-century drawings, paintings and sculpture.
Vejle is 30km (19 miles) north of Kolding and 75km (47 miles) southwest of Århus. Tourist office: Banegårdspladsen 6. Tel: 75 82 19 55; www.visitvejle.dk

Viborg

Viborg is one of Denmark's oldest cities, dating to the 8th century AD. It stands at a strategically important crossroads in central Jutland, midway between the Søndersø and Nørresø lakes. From the 11th to the 17th centuries it was the place where Danish monarchs were chosen and where they received the oath of allegiance from their subjects. It later declined, partly because of lack of access to the sea and partly because of the shift of political power to Copenhagen.

Viborg was also an important ecclesiastical centre, which accounts for the great twin-towered cathedral dominating the town. Only the crypt remains of the 12th-century church; after the ravages of fire and two centuries of neglect, the original building was demolished in 1863, and work on a huge new granite **cathedral** began the following decade. The interior is decorated with dazzling frescoes by Joakim Skovgaard. The candelabrum in front of the choir is also noteworthy.
81km (50 miles) south of Aalborg. Tourist office: Nytorv 9. Tel: 86 61 16 66; www.viborg.dk. Viborg Domkirke: Domkirkepladsen, Sankt Mogensgade 4. Tel: 87 25 52 58. Open: daily, Apr, May & Sept 11am–4pm; June–Aug 10am–5pm; Oct–Mar 11am–3pm. Free admission.

Political power left Viborg long ago, but the cathedral's twin towers still keep watch

Århus

With a population of around 286,000, Århus is Denmark's second city and the cultural capital of Jutland. Originally a Viking port and trading centre, it burgeoned in the 13th century when the cathedral was begun, fell into ruins two centuries later, and recovered in the 16th century when many of the city's fine buildings were constructed. The old and new blend harmoniously in Århus, which has some exemplary modern architecture and an atmospheric old town inhabited by a large and lively student community.

Traditional houses in the Old Town

Den Gamle By (The Old Town)

This is one of the best open-air museums in Denmark, with 75 reconstructed houses from all over the country set around a lakeside park. The purpose of the site is to demonstrate Danish village life from the 16th century through to the present by recreating domestic and working scenes down to the last detail. There are potters, blacksmiths and carpenters, all in period dress, busy at their workshops, as well as homes with displays of toys, textiles, watches and china. All that's missing for real authenticity is the traditional smell!

Viborgvej 2. Tel: 86 12 31 88; www.dengamleby.dk. Open: daily, Jan 11am–3pm; Feb, Mar, Nov & Dec 10am–4pm; Apr, May, Sept & Oct 10am–5pm; June–Aug 9am–6pm. Admission charge.

Domkirke (Cathedral)

Århus Cathedral – otherwise known as the Church of Saint Clement – is the longest church in Denmark, with a 93-m (305-ft) nave. The awesome interior has 15th-century frescoes by numerous different masters, and the vast altarpiece is one of the most ornate anywhere in the country.

The structure dates from the early 13th century, when a Romanesque church was built on the site. Four chapels off the chancel, and a few other portions, survive, but much of it was destroyed by fire. Much of today's Gothic cathedral dates from the rebuilding of 1450 to 1520.

Skt Clemens Gård, Skolegade 17. Tel: 86 20 54 00; www.aarhus-domkirke.dk. Open: daily, Oct–Apr 10am–3pm; May–Sept 9.30am–4pm. Free admission.

Forhistorisk Museum Moesgård (Moesgård Prehistoric Museum)

Set in an 18th-century manor house in the Moesgård woods, 5km (3 miles) south of the city centre (*see p120*), this is Denmark's most extensive and absorbing museum. Various periods in Denmark's prehistory (up to and including the Viking era) are illustrated by archaeological finds. One of the star attractions is the corpse of 'Grauballe Man' (*see pp118–19*). Among the several Viking exhibits are swords and coats of mail, of which reproductions have been made for visitors to handle and wear. There is also an interesting exhibition on the ethnography of Greenland (*see pp132–3*).

Moesgård Allé 20, Højbjerg.
Tel: 89 42 11 00.
Open: Apr–Sept, daily 10am–5pm;
Oct–Mar, Tue–Sun 10am–4pm.
Admission charge.
Bus No 6 (Moesgård).

Århus Tourist Office
Banegardspladsen 20. Tel: 87 31 50 10;
www.visitaarhus.com

Århus city plan (*see pp126–7 for walk route*)

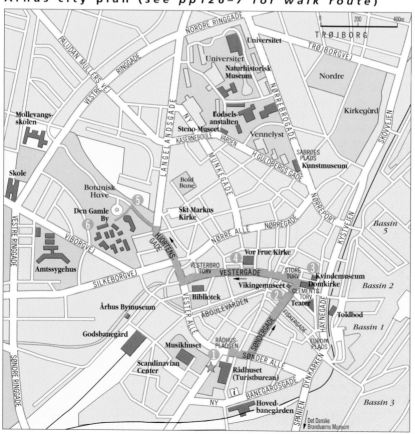

Kunstmuseet ARoS

Århus's newest art museum, opened in 2004, houses a fine collection of paintings, drawings and sculpture from the 18th century to the present, plus an outstanding array of work by cutting-edge Danish and international artists from the 1950s to the 21st century.
Aros Allee 2. Tel: 87 30 66 00;
www.aros.dk. Open: Tue–Sun
10am–5pm. Admission charge.

Musikhuset Århus (Concert Hall)

The Århus concert hall is one of Denmark's principal centres for the performing arts and home to the Århus Symphony Orchestra, the Danish National Opera and the Århus Festival. Built in 1982, it is both elegant and highly functional, having been acclaimed internationally for its fine acoustics.

There are two modern auditoriums, one of them with seating for over 1,000, and an airy foyer with plate-glass walls in which direct sunlight and indoor trees create an almost tropical effect. Ballet and opera performances, as well as classical and modern concerts, are held regularly in the main auditoriums, and exhibitions of art in the foyer. Even if there is little going on, the concert hall is worth visiting simply as an architectural sight.
Thomas Jensens Allé. Tel: 89 40 40 40;
www.musikhusetaarhus.dk.
Open: daily 11am–9pm, or later when
performances are being held.
Free admission, except to performances.

Århus Cathedral is the longest church in Denmark

The state-of-the-art Århus concert hall is an architectural wonder

Århus Bymuseum (Urban Museum)

Opened in 2006, the city's exciting new museum, in a definitively Danish modern building beside the river, centres around a permanent exhibition that portrays the development of Århus. There is a changing schedule of special exhibitions for children and adults.
Carl Blochs Gade 28. Tel: 86 13 28 62; www.bymuseet.dk. Open: daily 10am–5pm (until 8pm Wed). Admission charge.

Rådhuset (City Hall)

The City Hall is frequently described as an example of Danish design and architecture at its best. Modern, functional and clad in Norwegian marble, it is the work of Arne Jacobsen and was completed in 1941. The council chamber and civic hall are decorated with murals from the Nazi occupation, into which the artists slipped cryptic symbols of protest.

The most striking feature is the 60-m (197-ft) tower, from which there are superb views over the city.
Rådhuspladsen. Tel: 89 40 20 00. Guided tours in English, which include the bell tower, are conducted at 11am, Mon–Fri. Admission charge.

Steno-Danmarks Videnskabshistorisk Museet (Steno Museum)

This unusual and captivating museum, dedicated to the history of science and medicine, opened in 1994. A series of separate exhibitions begins on the ground floor with a collection of instruments used in astronomy, surveying, optics, magnetism, atomic and nuclear physics, chemistry, radio and computing – from Stone Age times, through the experimental physics of the 17th century, to the present day. Also on the ground floor is a parallel exhibition, charting the evolution of medicine from Hippocrates, in ancient Greece, through the invention of anaesthetics and X-ray, to a modern operating theatre.

Upstairs, a medicinal herb garden has been laid out on an outside terrace, based on herbs and substances described by Hendrik Smid in his 1546 *En Skjøn Lystig ny Urtegaard* (*An Attractive New Herb Garden*). The museum also has a planetarium, with shows at varying times on particular astronomical subjects. Some shows are specifically for children.
CF Møllers Alle 100, Universitetsparken. Tel: 89 42 39 75; www.stenomuseet.dk. Open: Tue–Fri 9am–4pm, Sat–Sun 11am–4pm. Admission charge.

Peat men

A group of peaceful peat-cutters from Grauballe (32km/20 miles west of Moesgård) got the shock of their lives one Saturday afternoon in 1952, when one of them struck a human head topped with reddish hair about half a metre (1½ft) below the surface. As they unearthed more of the naked body, they found, to their horror, that its throat had been slit from ear to ear.

At first, a recent murder was suspected. An autopsy was conducted by a professor of forensic medicine from Århus university. Fingerprints were taken by the Criminal Investigation Department. A dentist examined the corpse's 20 remaining teeth. The most revealing analysis, however, was the carbon dating which revealed the body to be approximately 2,000 years old.

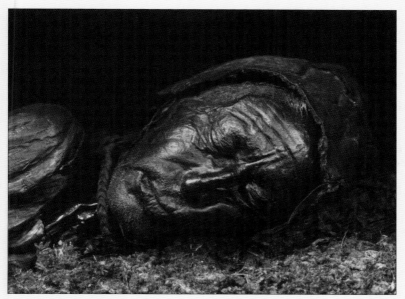

Because of the peat's chemical composition, the body had lain in a state of perfect preservation. According to the professor, its skin had undergone 'a process … which appears to resemble most closely a tanning.'

Between them, the experts managed to ascertain that the victim had been about 1.7m (5ft 7ins) tall, and in his mid-thirties at the time of his death. He was also unused to manual work. His left tibia had been broken and his throat cut, before his body was thrown into the bog. His last meal had been mainly of grain, although there were also indications that meat might have been included. He also suffered from intestinal worms. 'Grauballe Man', as he is known, is now the star attraction at the Moesgård Prehistoric Museum near Århus (*see pp114–15*) where he lies appearing to grin at his fascinated 21st-century visitors.

In the exhibition at Moesgård the death of the Grauballe Man has been interpreted as a human sacrifice. Several other bodies, including 'Tollund Man', have been discovered in the Jutland peat; many have met violent deaths. 'Tollund Man' died by strangulation, perhaps as a sacrificial victim, in about 220 BC and, like 'Grauballe Man', was preserved in a peat bog before being discovered in 1950.

'Grauballe Man' (opposite page) and 'Tollund Man' (above) rest in peace – as they have for the past 2,000 years or so

Walk: Moesgård

Moesgård is 5km (3 miles) south of Århus. This walk starts at the Prehistoric Museum and follows the so-called Prehistoric Trackway through a beautiful forest where ancient buildings have been reconstructed.

Allow 2 hours.

1 Forhistorisk Museum Moesgård (Moesgård Prehistoric Museum)

See pp114–15.
Follow the path that leads to the right of the museum, through gardens, past a lake on the left and through an apple orchard, into the open field of Monument Park.

2 Monument Park

The park is strewn with reconstructed prehistoric burial chambers and other monuments from all over Denmark, which, for varying reasons, have had to be moved from their original sites. Many of these are cist tombs, covered with slabs of stone, including the large and imposing Stone Age **Kobberup Cist**, the only one of its kind ever found. The

sheep, goats and ponies wandering the park are rare breeds closely related to those kept by the prehistoric inhabitants of Denmark.
From Monument Park a metalled road, shaded by beech, oak, ash and lime trees, leads down to the Skovmøllen.

3 Skovmøllen (Mill)

The beautifully half-timbered watermill has been turned into a restaurant serving traditional Danish food, as well as bread baked with home-ground flour. Ask inside to be shown the chunky old machinery, restored and functioning perfectly as the Giber Å (river) turns the wheel which grinds the grain.
Past the mill, turn left on to a footpath that passes a dolmen on the right before

entering and winding through the densest part of the forest. The trail emerges in an open field where the Tustrup temple stands.

4 Tustrup Huset (Temple)

Dating from about 2500 BC, this Stone Age structure is thought to have been used for religious rituals, with gifts of food brought to appease the spirits of the dead. The temple was discovered and excavated in 1954 at Tustrup, about 80km (50 miles) north of Moesgård. *The path joins a trackway along the edge of the beach. Turn left and follow this trackway to the fisherman's house at the mouth of the Giber Å (river). Turn left again, following the path that crosses to the north bank, via a footbridge, and leads to the Iron-Age House.*

5 Iron-Age House

This is a faithful reproduction of a house from the early Iron Age, constructed on the basis of a hut that was found at Tofting, just across the Danish border in Germany. The roof is supported by oak trunks, with shelter for the family at one end (next to a fire) and for their livestock at the other.

Immediately behind the house is an underground storage cellar, based on a cellar which was excavated at a different site, at **Grønheden** in north Jutland. *A footpath leads across a field back towards the Moesgård museum. Just beyond is the Viking Town.*

6 Viking Town

The reproduction Viking dwellings assembled here are based on those known from excavations in various regions of Denmark.

The main exhibit is the **Hedeby House**, which has a working oven. Visitors are sometimes offered a taste of home-made bread, with a swig of mead served in a stone cup.

Moesgård Prehistoric Museum
Moesgård Allé, Højbjerg. Tel: 89 42 11 00. Open: May–mid-Sept, daily 10am–5pm; mid-Sept–Apr, Tue–Sun noon–4pm. Admission charge.

Walk right into history at Moesgård

Walk: Aalborg

This stroll through old Aalborg starts at the heart of the city and takes in some historical sights before it comes to an end down at the fjord-side castle.
Allow 2 hours.

Start in Gammel Torv.

1 Rådhuset

The square in front of the town hall is the oldest part of the city. Distances from Aalborg are still measured from the stone column in the middle. The Rådhuset itself is not the same building that Jens Bang so famously sneered at (*see p89*), as this graceful yellow rococo edifice was not completed until 1762. Note the original gas lamps on either side of the entrance.
The façade of Jens Bang's house with the famous protruding tongue is opposite.

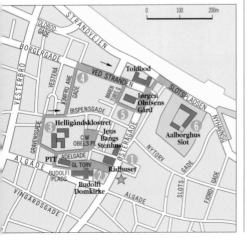

Cross the square and follow the sign to the cathedral.

2 Budolfi Domkirke

If you are here on the hour you will hear the carillon play (*see pp88–9*).
Pass the post office to the west of the cathedral, then turn down an alley leading into Adelgade. Turn right and follow the road into CW Obels Plads. On the square is the Helligåndsklostret.

3 Helligåndsklostret (Monastery of the Holy Ghost)

This former monastery is the oldest social institution in Denmark, dating from 1431. It was dedicated to the care of the elderly and infirm, and is still a home for 30 senior citizens. The conducted tour takes in a gloriously frescoed chapel and the monastic refectory.
Return to Adelgade, following the road down into the narrow and picturesque Latinergyrden (alley), emerging into pedestrianised Gravensgade. Turn right, then right again at the end of the road into Bispensgade, then second left into Jomfru Ane Gade.

4 Jomfru Ane Gade

This street is famous for its restaurants and cafés. There are about 30 along a

200-m (656-ft) stretch and there is always a great atmosphere here. If it is not lunch time, at least make this a beer or coffee stop.

Turn right into Ved Stranden and right again into Maren Turis Gade. No 6 is Jørgen Olufsen's Gård. Go in through this entrance (the house itself is not open to the public).

5 Jørgen Olufsens Gård

Built in 1616 by the wealthy Olufsen (Jens Bang's brother, *see p89*), there is probably no better-preserved merchant's house in Denmark. Note the hoists and doors to the grain lofts in the three-storey warehouse. In the gateway onto Østerågade, there is an original iron hook for weighing goods so that customers could check that they were not being cheated.

There is a second entrance on Østerågade. Exit the house here, turning immediately left, then right into the Slotspladsen, from where the castle comes into view.

6 Aalborghus Slot (Aalborg Castle)

King Christian III built this castle in the 16th century as a defensive fortress, but it was never needed for that purpose and became the official residence of the Lord Lieutenant, and so it

remains to this day. Access is confined to the courtyard, ramparts and dungeon.

Aalborg Castle
Tel: 99 30 60 90. Courtyard and ramparts open: 8am–sunset. Dungeon and underground passage open: May–Oct, Mon–Fri 8am–3pm. Free admission.
Monastery of the Holy Ghost
Tel: 99 30 60 90. Guided tours: daily, June–mid-Aug until 1.30pm. Admission charge.

Many of the old merchants' houses in the town are now used as offices

Tour: Limfjord

The Limfjord cuts a slim slice through the tip of Jutland, dividing the south of the peninsula and the northern extremity, where the landscape becomes more rugged. This drive takes you round the splintered inlets and islands, through some of the wildest countryside in Denmark.
Allow 5 hours.

1 Aalborg

Aalborg (*see p88*) was originally established as a Viking settlement, on account of its strategic position at the narrowest point on the Limfjord. The conurbation now straddles this stretch of water, together with its sister city Nørresundby on the northern side.
From central Aalborg follow the signs for Road No 187 towards Nibe, which is also called the Marguerite Route (see Driving, p180). Stay on this route, following the brown and white daisy signs, to skirt the

fjord, passing through Nibe and on to Løgstør.

2 Løgstør

The Limfjord Museum in the village demonstrates how closely the history of this town, as that of others on the fjord, is entwined with the herring industry, and with shipping and ferry traffic. The museum is in the former canal bailiff's house on the quayside facing on to the Frederik VII Canal.

The canal was built to bypass a

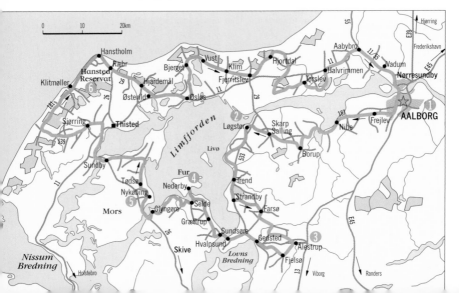

sandbar blocking one of the narrowest sounds on the Limfjord.
Continue along the Marguerite Route southwards, hugging the fjord, then turn sharply inland at Strandby, detouring to Ålestrup.

3 Ålestrup

There are two good reasons to stop here. One is to see the **Jydske Rosenpark** (Jutland Rose Garden) featuring more than 15,000 blooms and 200 different species. The other attraction here is the **Danmarks Cykelmuseum** (Bicycle Museum), with its display of about 100 different machines, from boneshakers to the latest in mountain bikes. Although Denmark is noted for both museums and cycling, this place is unique in combining the two.
Stay on the Marguerite Route to Hvalpsund, from where the ferry to Sundsøre takes 10 minutes and gives wonderful views across the fjord. Continue north along the waterside, taking a detour off the Marguerite Route at Selde for the five-minute ferry ride to Nederby, on Fur Island.

4 Fur Island

Fur is famous for its white clay, formed in part from fossilised algae and found nowhere else in the world except on nearby Mors Island. Cliffs of clay rise above the Limfjord, and a museum in Nederby demonstrates how this geological oddity was formed. The fossils on display include that of a giant turtle.
Return to the Marguerite Route and follow it to the junction with Road No 26 from Thisted to Skive. Turn sharp right

here and cross the bridge to Mors Island, turning right for Nykøbing.

5 Nykøbing

The beautiful Dueholm Kloster (monastery), founded in 1370, is located here. It houses a historical museum.
Follow the Marguerite Route back over the bridge from Mors Island and head for Thisted, bypass the town and continue west until you reach the coast. Follow the coast road north to Hansted Game Reserve.

6 Hansted Reservat

This is Denmark's most extensive wilderness – a National Reserve of woodland, bogs and sand dunes rich in birdlife. During the breeding season no one is allowed to enter the reserve on foot (*see p136*).
The Marguerite Route returns to the fjord at Østerild, where you continue eastwards via Fjerritslev, Hjortdal and Torslev. At Halvrimmen leave the route to take Road No 11 back to Nørresundby and Aalborg.

Limfjord Museum
*Kanalvejen 4. Tel: 98 67 18 05; www.limfjordsmuseet.dk.
Open: May–mid-June, Sept & Oct, Sat 2–5pm, Sun 10am–5pm; mid-June–Aug, daily 10am–5pm. Admission charge.*
Jydske Rosenpark
*Ålestrup. Tel: 98 64 23 86; www.rosenparken.dk.
Open: end-June–mid-Sept, daily 10am–8pm. Admission charge.*
Bicycle Museum
*Borgergade 10. Tel: 98 64 16 90; www.cykelmuseum.dk.
Open: May–Sept, daily 10am–5pm. Admission charge.*

Walk: Århus

This walk takes you through the heart of Århus,
taking in the historic centre of the town and some curious
museums. (*For map, see p115.*)
Allow 3 hours, not including time to explore Den Gamle By.

1 Rådhuspladsen
Dominating Town Hall Square is the
Rådhuset (*see p117*). In the middle of
the square is the large and amusing
sculpture of a sow and suckling piglets,
known as the **Pig Fountain**.

*Walk down pedestrianised Søndergade,
one of the city's main shopping streets,
until it reaches Clementstorv (square).
On the left is the Unibank building,
with the Viking Museum in the
basement.*

The simple, elegant interior of the Church of Our Lady

2 Vikingemuseet
(Viking Museum)

When the foundations were being dug for the Unibank building in 1964, the remains of the ramparts of a Viking village were discovered. Subsequently excavated, the site is now a small museum showing a section of the original ramparts and a reconstructed Viking home, complete with a loom, tools and utensils.

Outside the bank, turn right into Domkirkeplads, dominated by the great cathedral (see p114). Next to the cathedral (at No 5) is the unusual Kvindemuseet.

3 Kvindemuseet
(Women's Museum)

The small museum, located in a former police station, illustrates the traditional everyday lives of women in Denmark, and charts their 20th-century progress towards equality.

Behind the cathedral is a warren of cobbled streets known as the Latin Quarter. This is an area of boutiques and curiosity shops, bubbling with café life, particularly in term time. After a brief exploration, return to Domkirkepladsen. Pass the cathedral heading west to reach Store Torv, then continue straight on through Lille Torv and down Vestergade as far as the Vor Frue Kirke on the right.

4 Vor Frue Kirke
(Church of Our Lady)

This is the oldest structure in Århus, originally built by King Erik Ejegod in the 11th century. A former Dominican monastery, it survived the Reformation by instituting a hospital in the chapter house, which can be reached through a Gothic cloister. The nave is 14th century and the ornate altarpiece is 16th century. The real treat, however, is the vaulted crypt, which was discovered only during excavations as recently as the 1950s.

Continue down Vestergade and turn right at Vester Alle. Continue through Vesterbro Torv (square) and up Hjortensgade to the entrance to the Botanical Gardens.

5 Botanisk Have
(Botanical Gardens)

This large area of parkland is strewn with exotic shrubs and flowers. There are also several glasshouses containing more than 4,000 species of tropical and temperate plants.

Bear left through the gardens to the entrance to Den Gamle By (the Old Town).

6 Den Gamle By

This is Denmark's most extensive and authentic reconstructed old town (*see p114*). It makes for a fascinating visit and could easily absorb several hours of your time.

Viking Museum
Tel: 89 42 11 00. Open: Mon–Wed & Fri 10am–4pm; Thur 10am–5.30pm. Free admission.
Women's Museum
Tel: 86 18 64 70; www.kvindemuseet.dk. Open: Sept–May, Tue–Sun 10am–4pm; June–Aug, daily 10am–5pm. Admission charge.
Church of Our Lady
Tel: 86 12 12 43; www.aarhusvorfrue.dk. Open: May–Aug, Mon–Fri 10am–4pm, Sat 10am–noon; Sept–Apr, Mon–Fri 10am–2pm, Sat 10am–noon. Free admission.

Fishing

As a maritime nation, with both a North Sea and Baltic coastline, the history of the Danish people has always been closely bound up with fishing. Fish forms a substantial part of the Danish diet, whether fresh, frozen, smoked or soused. Fishing harbours punctuate the coastline. Some are huge ports, such as Esbjerg, but many more are tiny villages where fishing boats bob side by side with gleaming white yachts and sailing dinghies. The romance of the fisherman's life has a special place in the Danish psyche; the old salt with a bushy ginger beard, puffing a pipeful of tobacco, is still to be found on many a quayside.

The hard facts surrounding fishing in the modern world, however, tell a rather different story. Fishing has now become a massive global industry, and nations frequently come to blows over quotas, traditional fishing rights and territorial waters. Denmark has one of Europe's largest fleets, with some 2,000 boats of varying size, manned by around 6,000 fishermen. As well as fishing the Baltic and the North Sea, large ships bring catches back from the North Atlantic.

Even though the Danes are great fish eaters, nearly 90 per cent of the catch is exported, the bulk of it frozen or canned in giant fish-processing factories that can handle hundreds of thousands of tonnes of cod, plaice, mackerel and herring every year. In the same way as their counterparts working the land,

Danish fishermen have rationalised their industry, specialising in a few products which satisfy world demand, while maintaining a semblance of the romance bound up in their history.

For a fuller appreciation of this, it is worth visiting the Fiskeriog Søfartsmuseet (Fisheries and Maritime Museum) at Tarphagevej in Esbjerg (*see pp94–5*).

Fishing boats and their precious catch at Nørre Vorupor in Jutland

Getting away from it all

'Save in England, where else will you see so many acres of brilliant green lush meadow?' These words from Thomas Cook's *Traveller's Gazette* of 1904 still hold true today for Denmark, with its hundreds of nature reserves and parks. The verdant beauty of Denmark stretches, unusually for a country, from the eastern shores of the Atlantic Ocean to distant Greenland and the Faroe Islands, which open up to visitors in a brief burst of spring.

Sturdy wooden houses on the Faroe Islands

THE FAROE ISLANDS

The Faroes are among the most densely bird-inhabited islands in the world, stuck out in the wild North Atlantic, roughly halfway between Shetland and Greenland. Nobody knows exactly what the bird population of the islands must be, but the figure runs to some teeming millions: many birds spend only the warm months there, feasting on seafood, before they fly back south in winter in search of sunny climes. For the seabirds – constituting the majority of the bird population – this archipelago of 30 rugged, rocky humps and soaring cliffs must be something approaching an avian heaven.

Guillemots, kittiwakes, razorbills, cormorants, fulmars, gannets, oystercatchers and great skuas are just a few of the scores of winged species that nest in the cliffs, dive for fish and plankton and strafe the rocks with their bright, white droppings. Colonies of comical puffins with multicoloured beaks are also regular visitors; however, some of the more sentimental among the hundreds of birdwatchers who visit the islands between April and August are upset by the netting, plucking and cooking of these rare delicacies to please the Faroese palate.

More controversial still is the subject of whaling. The annual slaughter of hundreds of pilot whales that come to feed around the Faroese shores provokes arguments that are hard for visitors to ignore. 'Brutal,' say many conservationists; 'We do it sustainably, as we have done for generations,' counter the perpetrators. With the involvement of the likes of Greenpeace, the debate has taken on international proportions, and there are those who have been calling on tourists to boycott the islands and find somewhere else to get away from it all.

However, fishing and fish-processing, not whaling or puffin-catching, is the mainstay of Faroese life. Of the 45,500 people who live on 18 of the islands, nearly 17,000 live in **Tórshavn**, the capital, on Streymoy, the largest island. Tórshavn's busy little harbour has brightly painted houses and bobbing boats moored alongside larger vessels that form part of a huge fishing fleet. The rest of the island inhabitants are scattered in numerous coastal fishing villages or fjord-side settlements. A few live inland, farming the descendants of sheep brought to the islands by Irish monks in the 7th century. There are more than twice as many sheep as people on the islands, producing what some people believe to be the finest wool in the world. A few other farmers struggle against the odds with arable crops. Only 4 per cent of the land is cultivated and only one per cent of the population works in agriculture as a whole, because most of the land is rocky, windswept and unyielding, and harassed by the islands' extraordinarily capricious climate.

Without learning the lesson that the elements, not man, are supreme it is very hard to enjoy the Faroes. Hiking expeditions, fishing trips and inter-island boat journeys happen not according to some carefully worked out timetable, but when the weather allows. Even so, sun, rain and mist frequently replace each other in the course of just a few minutes, resulting in constant changes to the Faroese scenery.

The landscape consists of majestic mountains and dramatic ravines, bald hills, where scrubby grass is all that will grow, and forbidding cliffs that overlook surf that crashes hundreds of feet below. Standing as near to the edge as you dare, you can feel the buffeting wind, smell the salty tang in the air and watch a shaft of golden light break through the mist, while listening to the screeching of a million seabirds. It doesn't get much more bracing than the Faroes.

Faroes tour operators
Regent Holidays
31A High Street,
Shanklin, Isle of Wight
PO37 6JW.
Tel: 01983 864212.
For tourist information about the Faroes and Greenland, contact the Danish Tourist Board.

Tórshavn is a quaint little coastal town in the Faroe Islands

Island life

Most Greenlanders and Faroese make their first trip to Denmark as children. Among the many excitements of arriving in the motherland from these far-flung reaches of the kingdom is the prospect of seeing trees. Trees are just one of the wonders which they have previously only read or heard about. Other excitements are the commotion, noise and sheer scale of Copenhagen, which can induce utter bewilderment.

But emigration to sophisticated Europe is not a choice made by very many of these young people. A spell studying or a short period of work there, perhaps; but most conclude that the quality of life is better where they grew up. Can there be beauty without icebergs? Do not big skies and buffeting winds beat high-rise blocks and traffic?

Underpinning these typical sentiments, however, is the fact that the young people can also make a very good living back home. The economies of both Greenland and the Faroes are based on fishing and fish-processing.

By opting out of the European Union and its quotas, they have maintained favourable trading conditions.

In addition to this, there are large subsidies and entitlements to generous social security payments from Denmark, which suffers pangs of national guilt about the colonial past and its impact on the local island culture.

Greenland has only a few kilometres of road in total, but smart four-wheel drives are still commonplace. Fishermen and hunters come home to comfortable houses fitted with every modern convenience. Supermarkets in the main towns are stuffed with imported food, clothing and consumer goods. You can buy anything you want,

from designer Italian clothes to exotic tropical fruits.

Inuit people in Greenland living at the extremities of human endurance, or Nordic communities in the Faroes – both are rare examples in the modern world of traditional lifestyles being lived in harmony with the developed world's new prosperity and security. Some say they are having their (fish) cake and eating it, too.

Facing page: icebergs float in the sea around Greenland – very little of which is, in fact, green, and that too, only for a very short time in the year
Above: Tjornuvik Beach on Streymoy Island

MS *King of Scandinavia*

NORWAY AND SWEDEN

Denmark's nearest neighbours are just a short hop away by road, rail or ferry and are easy to combine with Denmark in a multi-centre holiday. Norway and Sweden – despite their strong cultural links with Denmark – offer a vastly different holiday experience, with scenic grandeur and wild, wide-open spaces that contrast strongly with the tidy, densely populated farmlands of the Danish countryside. Both Norway and Sweden offer a huge variety of landscapes, from Arctic snowfields to dense forests and rugged mountains, and both offer a huge choice of open-air holidays year-round, from fishing, hiking, sailing, kayaking and rafting in summer to dog-sledding, downhill and cross-country skiing and snowmobile travel in winter.

Both countries are easily accessible from Copenhagen, with SAS Scandinavian Airlines and other carriers offering frequent direct flights to gateway airports from the Baltic to the Arctic Circle.

From Copenhagen, Sweden is just minutes away across the amazing Øresund suspension bridge and tunnel, and it's possible to visit Sweden's pretty west coast for just a couple of days, or to venture onward by road and fast, efficient trains into a hinterland of lakes and rivers. By air, it's little over an hour from the heart of Copenhagen to the fringes of the Arctic Circle and the land of the summer midnight sun – or, in winter, to the home of Santa Claus, elves and reindeer.

Just across the narrow strait of the Kattegat, southern Sweden has two lively, cosmopolitan cities (Malmø and Gothenburg), a coastline of bays and

Kayaking in the Gothenburg archipelago

rocky offshore islands and a hinterland of forests, lakes and rivers where fishing, riding, canoeing and hiking are popular summer pastimes. Its gentler farming landscapes have been granted UNESCO World Heritage status, and its south-facing Baltic coast has miles of long sandy beaches that offer some of the best summer sunshine in Scandinavia. Norway offers an even bolder contrast with its southern neighbour, with few large cities and vast areas of wilderness. Only a few hours' sailing across the Skagerrak channel from Jutland, Norway's south coast is a region of bays, fjords and rocky islands while inland lie thick pine forests, fast-flowing rivers and steep mountains that rise to a region of rocky plateaux where reindeer roam and snow lies almost all year round. Kristiansand is the main port for

crossings to Norway from northern Denmark and is also the port of entry for ferries from the UK, which also sail to Gothenburg on the Swedish west coast. From here, it is possible to tour Norway by train, boat and bus, with a wide range of scenic journeys by land and water to choose from.

DFDS seaways
(*Tel: 08702 520 524; www.dfds.co.uk*) operates ferries and mini-cruises from Newcastle to Stavanger in Norway and Gothenburg in Sweden, and from Copenhagen to Helsingborg in Sweden. Rail Europe (*www.raileurope.co.uk*) sells a range of rail passes offering unlimited travel in Denmark, Norway and Sweden with discounted travel on ferry lines and buses.

Tourist information:
www.visitsweden.com
www.visitnorway.com

NATURE PARKS AND RESERVES
Amager Kalvebod Fælled
The piece of wilderness closest to central Copenhagen is this marshy wetland. Highly popular with bird spotters, the area also teems with insects and plenty of small mammal life – despite the aircraft noise.
About 5km (3 miles) south of Copenhagen, adjacent to Kastrup airport.

Draved Skov Nature Reserve
This reserve is an enchanting area of ancient, broad-leafed woodland. Trails for hikers and cyclists are waymarked through lime, oak and elm trees, whose stark winter beauty is transformed with carpets of wildflowers in spring, and the dense, darkening foliage of summer.

For many, the best time to visit is mellow, russet-and-yellow autumn, when locals forage the forest for wild mushrooms.
About 70km (43 miles) south of Esbjerg in the southwestern corner of Jutland, near the German border.

Farum Nature Park
City-dwelling nature lovers escape from Copenhagen to wander along this park's footpaths or to spot the rich birdlife and flora.
20km (12 miles) northwest of Copenhagen.

Hansted Nature Reserve
This important breeding ground for wetland birds is enclosed by the North Sea coastal road and the Limfjord shore (*see p125*).

Although admired and enjoyed by many motorists, particularly in the busy summer holiday season, there is no access to the reserve during the breeding season. Apart from marshes, the reserve encompasses sand dunes, open heathland and lakes.
Betweeen Klitmøller and Hantsholm in the far northwest of Jutland, beyond Limfjord.

Høje Møn Nature Park
Chalk cliffs rise dramatically out of the sea to a height of 128m (420ft) off the island of Møn (*see p52*). This nature park includes the forests that blanket the east of the island, ending abruptly at the cliff tops. Hiking and cycling trails wind through the undergrowth.
On the easern tip of Møn.

Nekselø Nature Reserve
The whole of the tiny island of Nekselø is designated as a nature reserve. Boats make the short crossing from the small harbour of Havnsø throughout the summer. The island's meadows and lakes contribute to an atmosphere entirely different from that of the rest of Zealand.
120km (75 miles) from Copenhagen off Zealand's northwestern coast.

Rands Fjord Nature Park
Despite its name, this 'fjord' is actually a freshwater lake, but is so-called because it was once connected to the sea on the eastern coast of Jutland. Footpaths lead around the lake, which is an important staging point for several species of wading birds, while wildfowl breed in the reed beds.
Southeast of Vejle (see p112), 6km (4 miles) beyond Børkop, on the road to Fredericia.

Rebild Bakker Nature Park

This park comprises the core of the **Rold Skov**, the most extensive area of woodland in Denmark, covering nearly 80sq km (31sq miles). It is also the richest in wildlife, home to red deer, roe deer, foxes, squirrels and martens. Nocturnal visitors might spot a badger and, occasionally, a wild boar.

As one of the country's hilliest regions, numerous streams trickle down from the high ground to feed a scattering of lakes and small ponds in the park. Some of the rarest flora in Denmark, including orchids not found anywhere else in the country, grow along their moistened banks.

By a curious quirk of history, this nature park owes its existence to a group of Danish-Americans whose parents emigrated in the 19th century. Wanting to keep alive their links with Denmark, they purchased a swathe of land in the Rebild hills ('bakker' is the Danish for hills) and presented it to the Danish people in 1912, on condition that it should remain a nature park forever.

About 25km (16 miles) south of Aalborg, on the road to Hobro.

Birdwatching near Rands Fjord Nature Park

An increasingly rare sighting: red deer

Rømø Nature Reserve

Although only part of the island is designated as a nature reserve, the whole of Rømø enjoys an atmosphere of isolation. To the north, grassy meadows and sand dunes sweep down in an arc to the south. The central areas rise to heathland, while the eastern side, looking across the flats to mainland Jutland, is alive with migratory wading birds in the spring and autumn.

The greatest treat for birdwatchers, however, is in July and August, when they can see the thousands of avocets which arrive here to breed, departing with the onset of autumn.

Rømø island is joined to mainland Jutland via a 9-km (5½-mile) causeway built across the tidal mud and sand flats. It is reached by taking the A12 south from Esbjerg, then turning right for the causeway in the town of Skaerbaek.

Skagen Nature Park

Up on the tip of Jutland, this park is Denmark's wildest area, the point where the peninsula meets the Skagerrak and Kattegat seas. Access to the park is unrestricted throughout the year, and trails pass through wind-buffeted sand dunes, heathland and conifer forests.

Skagen is also a key spot to observe migrating birds, especially between April and June when thrushes and finches fly northwards in huge numbers on their way to Norway and Sweden.

The park is reached by driving north from Aalborg as far as you can go, past Frederikshavn and Skagen.

Skallingen Nature Reserve

The views are best from the northern stretch of the peninsula: in autumn you can look out over the wetlands to observe thousands of pairs of eider duck and dunlin, as well as rare pink-footed geese and greenshanks. In summer, you can see the occasional ruff.

Located on a 10-km (6-mile) long peninsula of marshes and sand dunes facing the North Sea, 20km (12 miles) west of Esbjerg. Reached along a narrow road from the village of Ho.

Tipperne Nature Reserve

There is no public access to the central part of the reserve, although there is an information centre and observation tower (access restricted to 1–5pm on Wednesdays, Fridays and Sundays in June and July). Birdlife can also be observed from footpaths around the periphery.

Dunlin and wigeon breed here in profusion; up to 5,000 pairs of Bewick's swans may arrive here in winter. To the

south of the reserve is a popular hunting area; wildfowling is permitted from 15 October to early spring.
Located on a small peninsula at the southern end of the Ringkøbing Fjord. It can be reached by road from Esbjerg via Varde or Billum, turning right just before Nyminde.

Tistrup-Bavelse Nature Park
The woodlands and meadows of this extensive park are dotted with prehistoric monuments, as well as lakes and marshes where wildfowl breed in winter.

Located between Ringsted and Fuglebjerg in southwestern Zealand.

Utterslev Mose Nature Reserve
This shallow, marshy lake and its surrounding parkland is a peaceful haven rich in birdlife, despite the road bridges (including a four-lane highway) that cross it. Water channels cut through the expanses of reeds and marsh where wildfowl nest. Footpaths and cycle tracks skirt the perimeter.
6km (4 miles) from central Copenhagen. Bus 68 from Rådhuspladsen drops you within a couple of minutes of the reserve.

Wild Skagen Nature Park is buffeted by winds from the Baltic and North Seas

Tradition preserved intact in the remote islands

REMOTE ISLANDS

Nature has made Danes into a nation of bridge builders: they are world leaders in bridge design and engineering, having linked up many of the islands that constitute Denmark. For example, Funen is linked to Jutland, and Zealand is linked, in turn, to Funen and southern Sweden. Bridges further link both these islands to several smaller islands in their respective archipelagos.

However, there are still a number of very remote islands whose inviolable isolation and sense of true insularity are part of their special charm.

Læsø, out in the Kattegat (1½ hours by ferry from Frederikshavn in North Jutland), is a tranquil haven of woodland and heath, sand dunes speckled with marram grass, salt marshes rich in wildlife and long, exposed beaches. The resident population is just 2,300, and most of them live in the port of Vesterø Havn, where the ferry lands, or in Byrum, the main town.

Samsø is a popular holiday isle for nature lovers who rent homes there to enjoy the beaches, and cycle through the forests and meadows. Samsø is almost equidistant from Jutland, Zealand and Funen, and accessible by ferry from Jutland and Zealand. Though roughly the same size as Læsø, Samsø has a larger population.

Tiny **Anholt** (a mere 22sq km/

8½sq miles), about halfway between Jutland and Sweden, is made up of sand dunes, beaches and plains, and has banned all motor vehicles. Occupied by the British Navy during the Napoleonic Wars (when it was known as HMS *Anholt*), the island has prospered in more peaceful times. The 150 islanders welcome small numbers of visitors each summer, mainly as paying guests in their own homes, although there is an inn and a campsite. A 2½-hour journey by ferry takes visitors from Grenå, in east Jutland, to the island.

Læsø, an island that appeals to 'Robinson Crusoe' types

S h o p p i n g

Silverware is among the more expensive souvenir items that can be bought

Denmark is no place for bargain-hunters. Instead, the joy of shopping in Copenhagen and other Danish cities is the range of high-quality goods on offer, presented in the style for which the country is famous. For serious purchases of the best in Danish design, your pocket needs to be deep; non-EU residents, however, can mitigate the expense on substantial purchases by asking for a refund of the 25 per cent Value Added Tax (*see box below*).

Amber
Amber – fossilised resin – washes up on Baltic beaches and has been worked into jewellery by the Danes for centuries, being sold as earrings, necklaces and other trinkets all over Denmark.

Candles
Danes are incorrigible candle-burners, with flickering flames adorning every meal table, including breakfast.

VAT refunds
Danish prices include 25 per cent VAT, known as MOMS, which amounts to 20 per cent of the total price. This is refundable to non-EU residents at the airport, provided Denmark is the last stop before travelling to a non-EU destination.

The rate of refund is between 15 per cent and 19 per cent of the total price, depending on the amount. Ask for a tax-free receipt at the point of purchase on a purchase of over 300Dkr. This must be stamped by the customs authorities in Terminal 3 before you check in your baggage and cashed at the VAT Refund desk in the Transit Hall.

For further information contact: Global Refund Danmark A/S.
Tel: 32 52 55 66; www.globalrefund.com

Appropriately, candle-making is something of an art form in Denmark and candles come in all shapes, sizes and designs. Many department stores and gift boutiques stock a huge range of candles and candle holders in traditional and avant-garde designs. Both make excellent gifts or souvenirs.

Clothing
Danes are keen followers of fashion, as opposed to avant-garde innovators, so it is hardly surprising that cool clothes are easy to come by in the main towns and cities. Clothes are, however, comparatively expensive here although there are several chain stores in which bargains can be found. Naturally, Copenhagen is the country's fashion centre, home to numerous inter-nationally renowned designers and stores. This is the place to come to find upcoming trends and styles. Less trendy, but eminently practical, is Danish knitwear, particularly woollen sweaters, which are a Scandinavian speciality. Good buys can be found all over the country. Denmark and Greenland also

have a thriving fur industry and furs are worn during winter without fear of retribution from animal rights activists. For Danes a fur is a practical – some might say essential – part of a winter wardrobe.

Glass

There are several modern Danish glassblowers who have combined their ancient craft with progressive design ideas. Holmegaard of Copenhagen, on Copenhagen's Østergade 15–17 (part of Strøget walking street), is the most famous producer. There is a museum of glass in Ebeltoft (*see p94*).

Hi-fi equipment

The ultra-sleek designs of Bang & Olufsen are among Denmark's most renowned exports. The company has centres displaying the latest equipment in several Danish cities; in Copenhagen they are at Østergade 3–5 on Strøget.

Porcelain

Royal Copenhagen and Bing & Grøndal are the two best-known names in Danish porcelain. Both now belong to the same company, but maintain distinct styles. You can take a tour of the Royal Copenhagen factory, in Frederiksberg, Copenhagen.

Bric-a-brac galore in Copenhagen's flea markets, held during the summer months

Street musicians can entertain you while you shop at a leisurely pace

COPENHAGEN

The pedestrianised Strøget or 'Promenade' – actually five different but consecutive streets – is over 1km (⅔ mile) long and is the main shopping focus in the capital, with hundreds of outlets ranging from tawdry tourist boutiques to Denmark's most stylish shops. A short bus ride away in the Nørrebro area of town you will find the city's antiques quarter, centred on the street Ravnsborggade.

A selection of shops is listed here:

Danske Mobelkunst
Classic but expensive Danish furniture from leading designers such as Arne Jacobsen, Poul Henningsen and Kaare Klint.
Bredgade 32.

Georg Jensen
Denmark's most famous silversmith, selling key rings to jewellery.
Amagertorv 4, Strøget.
www.georgjensen.com

Hennes & Mauritz
Bargain-basement but still trendy clothing in this huge, multi-level flagship store.
Amagertorv 23, Strøget. www.hm.com

Illum and Magasin du Nord
There is little to choose between Copenhagen's two great department stores. Both have an impressive range of clothes, food, cosmetics, interior design items and household goods. Both are situated in the centre of town.
Illum: Østergade 52, Strøget.
Magasin du Nord: Kongens Nytorv 13.

Illums Bolighus
The perfect showcase for the best of Danish and international interior design, with everything from beds to bags, dressers to dressing gowns.
Amagertorv 10, Strøget. www.illum.dk

Rosenthal Studio-Haus
Wonderful showroom featuring porcelain, glassware, vases, cutlery and kitchen goods from top designers.
Frederiksberggade 21.
www.rosenthal.dk

Royal Copenhagen Porcelain
The historic porcelain manufacturer's flagship store, in the heart of Strøget.
Amagertorv 6, Strøget.
www.royalcopenhagen.com

Sweater Market
Stocks a huge range of hand-knitted Scandinavian pure wool sweaters in traditional and classical designs. Many come with matching accessories, such as caps, scarves, gloves and socks.
Nytorv 19, Strøget.
www.sweatermarket.dk

Sølvkælderen
A cellar shop on a pedestrian street parallel to Strøget, selling a fabulous array of antique silverware.
Kompagnistræde 1.

AALBORG

Lange Handicrafts

A city-centre shop with an old farmhouse atmosphere, selling a good selection of stoneware, china and glass, and mounting handicraft demonstrations in its workshop.
Hjelmerstald 15.

ODENSE

Rosendgårdcentret

Denmark's biggest shopping centre has everything you could wish to buy, from interior design to electronics, handicrafts, food and clothing. There are also restaurants and a cinema.
Rosendgårdcentret, Blå Gade 3.
Tel: 66 15 91 18.

Inspiration Zinck

Fashionable and beautiful interior design and handicrafts. The widest selection on Fyn.
Vestergade 82–84. Tel: 66 12 96 93.

ÅRHUS

Galleriværkstedet

Over 630sq m (6,780sq ft) of Danish art including glassware, ceramics, paintings and sculpture. A beautiful browse even if you have no intention of buying.
Studsgade 44. Tel: 86 13 77 76;
www.habsoe.dk

Museums Kopi Smykker

Working together with Danish and overseas museums, Museums Kopi Smykker crafts perfect replicas of ancient jewellery in gold, silver and bronze.
Kannikegade 12. Tel: 86 12 76 88.

Salling

A top-quality department store, with 30 specialist shops under one roof, including jewellery, designer clothing, china, glass and handicrafts.
Søndergade 27. www.salling.dk

Busy shopping streets are inviting enough to tempt even the most reluctant

Danish design

If one company embodies the design pre-eminence that Denmark has claimed since the 1950s, it is Bang & Olufsen. The company's sleek, high-tech television sets and hi-fi equipment are in demand as status symbols all over the world. Significantly, the electronic components are made by Japanese and other foreign firms. Denmark has chosen not to compete at the cutting edge of electronic innovation. What it does offer is a flair for design. Importing the technology allows Bang & Olufsen to combine outstanding design quality with technical excellence.

Furniture, glassware, porcelain, cutlery, jewellery, silverware, lighting and architecture are other areas in which Danish designers have been setting world trends in recent decades. The explanation for this phenomenon probably lies in a combination of the highly developed crafts which already existed in Denmark before World War II, and the national mood after 1945, which looked forward in rather the same way as the defeated nations did, rather than resting on the laurels of victory and history.

Simplicity became a theme, as the functionalism of the pre-war years was combined with a sense of aesthetics. Why should not everyday objects such as tables, chairs, knives and forks, for

Visible everywhere – from sleek, hi-tech electronics (above) to modern architecture (facing page). The Radisson was designed by Arne Jacobsen, godfather of Danish design

example, be both practical and beautiful? In many parts of Europe, especially Britain, the concept of beauty in design is still anchored to the concept of the antique, but Danish designers have bounded off into pastures new.

Ironically, some of the classic Danish designs of the 1950s and '60s have now assumed a sort of 'antique' value of their own – enough for them to be collected and displayed in museums around the world.

Entertainment

COPENHAGEN

Copenhagen is the most vibrant city in Scandinavia, with an immensely varied year-round entertainment programme and a nightlife that ranges from the cosy to the throbbing, and which lasts until dawn. Throughout the summer, street entertainment is an inescapable feature of the city. Along the Strøget and elsewhere, musicians – classical, folk and modern – as well as jugglers, acrobats and clowns lend Copenhagen a carnival atmosphere that can add to the enjoyment of drinking at the numerous outdoor cafés.

For listings of concerts and cultural events, visit the *Wonderful Copenhagen* website at *www.visitcopenhagen.dk* or pick up a copy of *Copenhagen This Week* from the tourist office. Live music is played at many venues, and jazz is particularly popular in the capital. The July Copenhagen Jazz Festival is world famous.

Cinemas

New-release English-language films reach Denmark quickly; they are almost invariably shown with the original soundtrack and Danish subtitles. Listings are found in daily newspapers and at *www.aok.dk*

Almost like a palace, Palads is a royal experience

Grand

Good for populist art-house pictures.
Mikkel Bryggersgade 8.
Tel: 33 15 16 11.

Imperial

Worth going to see anything here just for the experience of viewing the vast screen, which some say is the largest in Europe.
Ved Vesterport 4.
Tel: 70 13 12 11.

Palads

A large multiplex with numerous different screens showing the newest releases.
Alex Torv 9.
Tel: 70 13 12 11.

Classical music

Radiohusets Koncertsal

The main venue for classical concerts.
Julius Thomsensgade 1.
Tel: 35 20 62 62.

Clubs

Copenhagen is at the heart of northern European youth culture, but its clubs still follow trends rather than set them. However, their relaxed atmosphere more than compensates.

Club Cavi

This is an extremely stylish lounge bar and club with large outside

Live music is played at many venues

terrace, three bars and a dance floor.
Lille Kongensgade 16.
Tel: 33 11 20 20.

Park

A popular, unpretentious nightclub with lavish faux-Renaissance style interior. Located outside the city centre in Østerbro.
Østerbrogade 79.
Tel: 35 42 62 48.

Rust

The trendsetter on the Copenhagen club scene. Very cool and very contemporary.
Guldbergsgade 8,
Nørrebro.
Tel: 35 24 52 00.

Vega

The number one night-time destination in Copenhagen boasts two club venues plus a lounge and bars. Attracts major international DJs.
Enghavevej 40, Vesterbro.
Tel: 33 25 70 11.

Live music

Copenhagen Jazz House

Great atmosphere: Denmark's number one jazz venue.
Neils Hemmingsgade 10.
Tel: 33 15 26 00.

Den Grå Hal

The hippy commune Christiania's main live music venue, Den Grå Hal attracts internationally known rock and pop stars, as well as big Danish names and newcomers.
Christiania,
Christianshavn.
Tel: 32 54 31 35.

Copenhagen's Royal Theatre, Det Kongelige Teater

Drop Inn
Intimate, friendly jazz
and blues venue, close
to the Town Hall
Square.
Kompagnistræde 11.
Tel: 33 11 24 04.
Mojo
Good solid blues and
rock.

Løngangsstræde 21c.
Tel: 33 11 64 53.
Pumpehuset
A large-capacity music
venue based in a
converted power station.
Attracts major
international names.
Studiestræde 52, Vesterbro.
Tel: 33 93 19 60.

Vega
David Bowie, Suede,
Bryan Adams, Bjork and
Fatboy Slim are among
the artists who have
played at this top
night spot.
Engehavevej 40,
Vesterbro.
Tel: 33 25 70 11.

Theatre, opera and ballet

Det Kongelige Teater
Denmark's main opera and ballet venue, plus theatrical performances.
Kongens Nytorv 9.
Tel: 33 69 69 33.

Opera Copenhagen
Having opened in January 2005 on a harbour site facing the Royal Palace, at a cost of Dkr 2.4 billion, Europe's newest opera house is home to the national opera company, with a programme two-thirds opera, one-third ballet.
Tel: 33 69 69 78.

OUTSIDE COPENHAGEN

The entertainment scene away from Copenhagen pales in comparison with the capital. Nevertheless, the night owl will find lively nocturnal activities in the university city of Århus, particularly during term time, and in Odense and Aalborg. All three also have their own symphony orchestras.

Aalborg
Most of Aalborg's nightlife is concentrated on Jomfru Ane Gade, the vibrant, pedestrianised street between Bispengade and Borgergade, which is lined with restaurants, cafés, bars and discos.

Aalborg Kongres og Kultur Center
The city's main culture centre staging events of all kinds, from boxing to classical concerts.
Europa Plads 4.
Tel: 99 35 55 66.

Some of the world's best ballet can be seen in Denmark

John Bull Pub
Lively atmosphere and
live music at weekends.
Highly recommended.
Østeragade 20.
Tel: 98 11 57 88.

Skråen
A café and multiscreen
cinema that also features
concerts by local bands.
Strandvejen 19.
Tel: 98 12 21 89.

Esbjerg
Esbjerg's vibrant disco
and live music scene is
mostly to be found
around Torvet, the main
square.

Open-air rock concerts are held regularly throughout the summer in Copenhagen

Dronning Louise
Restaurant, bar and
nightclub with live
music, catering for a
more mature audience.
Torvet 19. Tel: 75 13 13 44.

Esbjerg Teater
Stages Danish (and
occasionally English)
productions.
Komgensgade 34.
Tel: 75 45 30 55.

Musikhuset
Esbjerg's main concert
hall, designed by
legendary architect Jørn
Utzon of Sydney Opera
House fame.
Havnegade 48.
Tel: 76 10 90 00.

Strandbio
Five-screen cinema
showing recent English-
language releases.
Strandbyplads 7.
Tel: 75 12 15 07.

Tobakken
Purpose-built live music
venue with regular rock,
jazz and theatrical
performances.
Gasværksgade 2.
Tel: 75 18 00 00.

Odense
Visit *www.visitodense.com*
for the latest on things to
do in Odense. Through-
out the annual summer
jazz festival, there are free
outdoor concerts.

Alibi Supper Club
Restaurant, music café
and nightclub, live
concert venue.
Brandts Passage 37.
Tel: 66 14 82 99.

Badstuen
Musicians of alternative
persuasion are usually to
be found at this radical
haunt.
Østre Stationvej 26.
Tel: 66 13 48 66.

Late-night revellers live it up

Boogie Dance Café
Popular dance spot
beneath Birdies café.
Nørregade 21.
Tel: 66 14 00 39.

Café Oscar
A wide variety of
musicians, including folk
singers.
Vestergade 75.
Tel: 66 14 25 35.

Dexter
Lively bar with buffet
food and live jazz.
Vindegade 65.
Tel: 66 13 68 88.

Musik Koelderen
This is the most popular

jazz and blues venue in
Odense.
Dronningensgade 2b.
Tel: 65 91 40 60.

Rytmeposten
Loud music mainly from
the local rock bands in
this converted post office.
Østre Stationvej 27a.
Tel: 66 13 60 20.

Århus
To find out what's on in
Århus, visit
www.visitaarhus.com

Århus Teater
This old-established
theatre has four separate

stages – a main one
where classical drama
is performed, and three
smaller ones for fringe
performances.
Bispetorvet.
Tel: 86 12 26 22.

Cinemaxx Århus
New multi-screen
complex showing the
latest English-language
releases.
Brauns Galleri,
Braunsgade 25.
Tel: 70 12 01 01.

Fatter Eskil
Mainly blues, but
sometimes hosts more

modern jazz bands.
Skolegade 25.
Tel: 86 19 44 11.
Jazzbar Bent J
Small, lively jazz bar
that stays open late.
Nørre Allé 66.
Tel: 86 12 04 92.
Musikhuset Århus
The city's magnificently
stylish concert hall stages
a wide variety of classical
concerts year round, plus
opera, jazz, rock bands
and other forms of
entertainment.
Thomas Jensens Allé.

Tel: 86 12 12 33.
Romer
Århus's newest and
hippest café-nightclub
with resident DJs and
cutting-edge sounds.
Aboulevarden 50.
Tel: 86 12 03 30;
www.caferomer.dk
Social Club
Newly renovated venue
playing mainstream and
chart hits on two dance
floors – the best club in
Århus.
Klosterport 34.
Tel: 86 19 42 50.

Train
This is one of Denmark's
most respected and
largest music venues
and it attracts popular
rock, pop and jazz
acts from around the
world.
Toldbodgade 6.
Tel: 86 13 47 22.
Voxhall
Excellent live music
venue – features
everything from
techno to jazz music.
Vester Alle 15.
Tel: 87 30 97 97.

Drummers at Copenhagen Harbour Festival

Children

All over Denmark, a wide variety of children's activities is available to suit all ages. Many museums and tourist attractions have a play area or a special exhibition for youngsters. These keep children amused so that their parents get the most out of their sightseeing. Similarly, hotels and restaurants nearly all have cots, highchairs and special menus. The one ingredient that parents might find lacking is a sense of warmth towards children. Every juvenile need is catered for, but Danish reserve is such that children are rarely made a fuss of.

Tivoli World, North Jutland

Activity parks

'Sommerlands' commercially run parks, found in many parts of Denmark, offer a wide variety of water- and land-based activities, such as water chutes, water cycles, rafts, pony rides, go-karting and shooting ranges.
Contact tourist offices for information (see p188).

Legoland

This is undoubtedly one of the best children's attractions in northern Europe (*see pp104–5*).

Safari Park

Knuthenborg Safari Park, on the island of Lolland, features more than 900 animals from around the world. There is also a small zoo especially for young children.
*Godskontoret, Birketvej 1, DK-4941 Bandholm. Tel: 54 78 80 89; www.knuthenborg.dk.
Open: May–Oct, daily 9am–5pm. Admission charge.*

Tivoli Friheden

This large amusement park is near the centre of Århus and is set in a beautiful park. Open-air concerts in summer.
Skovbrynet, Århus. Tel: 86 14 73 00; www.friheden.dk. Open: daily, July & Aug 1–11pm, until 10pm in June. Shorter hours Apr–May & Sept, see website for details. Admission charge.

Tivoli Gardens

No trip to Copenhagen is complete without a visit to Tivoli Gardens, which are particularly thrilling for children, and especially at night (*see p38*).

Tivoli Karolinelund Aalborg

The largest amusement park in North Jutland. A large funfair, within walking distance of the city centre, with exciting rides and popular fairytale figures wandering around.
Aalborg. Tel: 98 12 33 15; www.tivoliland.dk. Open: daily, Apr, Aug & Sept noon–8pm; May & June noon–9pm; July 10.30am–10pm. Admission charge.

Zoos

Aalborg

Good open spaces (for both animals and visitors) in this imaginatively sculpted landscape.

Mølleparkvej 63. Tel: 96 31 29 29;
www.aalborg-zoo.dk.
Open: daily, end Mar–Apr 10am–4pm,
May–Aug 9am–6pm, Sept & Oct
10am–4pm, Nov–Mar 10am–2pm.
Admission charge.

Copenhagen

This has a good selection of animals, with a special mini-zoo for small children and a new Tropical Zoo.

Roskildevej 32. Tel: 72 20 02 00;
www.zoo.dk. Open: daily, Jan–Mar, Nov
& Dec 9am–4pm; Apr, May, Sept & Oct,
9am–5pm; June–Aug 9am–6pm.
Admission charge.

Odense

This is the second-largest zoo in Denmark.

Sdr Boulvard 306. Tel: 66 11 13 60;
www.odensezoo.dk. Open: Nov–late Mar,
daily 9am–4pm; late Mar–Apr, Sept &
Oct, Mon–Fri 9am–5pm, Sat & Sun
9am–6pm; May–June & Aug, Mon–Fri
9am–6pm, Sat & Sun 9am–7pm; July,
daily 9am–7pm. Admission charge.

Kiddie cars at Tivoli Gardens

Sport and leisure

Danes are keen sports players and spectators, with a particular passion for football. The continued success of the Danish national team in the World Cup and the worldwide reputations of a handful of Danish players have added to this. Two other sports in which Denmark is prominent are badminton and sailing. A wide variety of participant and spectator sports can be enjoyed by visitors to Denmark.

An angler enjoying a bit of solitude at sundown near Assens

Angling

A licence must be obtained to fish in natural waters in and around Denmark. The licence is valid for a year and can be purchased from Danish post offices or larger fishing-tackle shops. Weekly and daily licences are also available for 75Dkr and 25Dkr respectively. Those aged under 18 or over 65 are exempt from the licence.

Fishing rights in natural lakes and streams are almost invariably private but are often contracted to local angling societies which issue day or week cards. In addition to the fishing licence described above, rates are around 40–150Dkr for a day card and 100–300Dkr for a week card. In many places, boats can be rented with fishing rights included. Often, these cards are available from local tourist offices who also have details of the freshwater fishing possibilities in the area.

For sea fishing, nearly all stretches of Denmark's 7,500-km (4,660-mile) coastline are accessible to the public as long as there is a passable beach between the sea and cultivated land. The coast must be approached by a public road only. Anglers may not take up position within 50m (164ft) of a public house. A licence is required as already detailed but no other special permission is needed. For safety reasons, jetty fishing is prohibited at several places on the North Sea coast.

In many Danish harbours, fishing boats will take anglers out to sea for a reasonable charge. Larger groups can charter a boat for themselves. Sea-fishing tours are arranged throughout the year from Copenhagen, Helsingør, Korsør and Frederikshavn. From other harbours, there are usually tours in the summer months only. A fishing licence, but no other form of permission, is needed.

For information and addresses of local angling societies contact:
Danmarks Sportsfiskerforbund
Worsåesgade 1, DK-7100 Vejle.
Tel: 75 82 06 99; www.sportsfiskeren.dk

Athletics

Athletics meetings are held in Denmark all the year round, and many of them are open to foreign entrants.

One of the best-known annual events is the **Copenhagen Marathon**, which takes place in May.

For further information contact:

Idrættens Hus
Brøndby Stadion 20, DK-2605 Brøndby. Tel: 43 26 29 10.

Badminton

Badminton is an extremely popular sport in Denmark and most of the major towns have excellent indoor courts. These are often in heavy demand and it can be difficult to find courts available. Generally, mornings are the easiest time to get in.

For further information, including details about training camps and tuition, contact:

Dansk Badminton Forbund
Idrættens Hus, Brøndby Stadion 20, DK-2605 Brøndby. Tel: 43 26 29 10.

Cycling

With its gentle undulations and extensive network of well-maintained cycle tracks, Denmark is a superb cycling country.

The Danish Cyclists' Association furthers the cause of all kinds of cycling. It publishes several leaflets which are useful in the planning of a cycling holiday, such as *Cycle Tracks in Denmark*, together with route maps covering the country. Their excellent website should be the first stop for anyone considering a cycling holiday in Denmark.

Cycling is one of the most popular leisure activities

For further information contact:
Dansk Cyclist Forbund
Rømersgade 7, DK-1362, Copenhagen K. Tel: 33 32 31 21; www.dcf.dk
Many local tourist offices also offer inclusive cycling holidays which can be prepaid, with arrangements made in advance. The holiday will include the rent of bicycles and carriers, detailed route descriptions, with maps and ferry tickets if required, plus overnight accommodation. There are reductions if you bring your own bicycle. The routes are all laid out by local experts, ensuring that, whenever possible, they follow good cycle tracks and little-used minor roads. Contact any Danish tourist office (in Denmark or abroad) for details about these excellent holidays.

Football

With some 300,000 active players, this is the one sport that excites Denmark above all others.

For details of major venues, where top club and international matches are played, contact:
Dansk Boldspil-Union
Idrættens Hus, Brøndby Stadion 20, 2605 Brøndby. Tel: 43 26 22 22; www.dbu.dk

Golf

The rolling Danish countryside is ideal for golf and there are currently 117 courses spread across the country. Foreign visitors are welcome at Danish clubs and typically find them to be less fussy and pretentious than clubs in the UK and USA. Some clubs have introduced handicap restrictions, so it is a good idea to check with the club pro

or secretary before visiting. Green fees are reasonable, at around 200Dkr for 18 holes on weekdays, and around 300Dkr at weekends. Courses near large cities can be crowded on weekends and holidays.

For lists of courses, green fees and information on golfing holidays contact:
Dansk Golf Union
Idrættens Hus, Brøndby Stadion 20, DK-2605 Brøndby. Tel: 43 26 27 00; www.dgu-golf.dk

Horse riding

There are riding schools, stables and centres throughout Denmark, some of which offer special riding holidays with half or full board. Prices per hour are from around 70Dkr, and up to 200Dkr if tuition is included; day hire rates are 200–600Dkr. At many centres, horse-drawn wagons can also be hired.

For further information contact:
Dansk Ride Forbund
Idrættens Hus, Brøndby Stadion 20, DK-2605 Brøndby. Tel: 43 26 28 11; www.rideforbund.dk

Sailing

With Denmark's wealth of harbours and marinas, the country offers excellent sailing facilities. Most visitors who come to Denmark specifically for a sailing holiday sail or tow their own boats.

For lists of companies offering boat hire contact:
Dansk Sejlunion
Idrættens Hus, Brøndby Stadion 20, DK-2605 Brøndby. Tel: 43 26 21 82; www.sejlsport.dk. (Always bring certificates of competence to sail particular classes of boat.)

Tennis

Tennis is so popular all year round in Denmark that most clubs' courts, both indoor and outdoor, are fully booked by members after 5pm. If you feel like a game, make sure you contact clubs in advance, since many clubs welcome guests, particularly during the lean off-peak hours.

Hire costs are usually around 125Dkr for outdoor courts and 150Dkr for indoor. Most holiday and sports centres have courts which are more accessible and either free or relatively cheap. In most cases it is also possible to rent or borrow racquets, balls and shoes.

During the summer, grand-prix tennis tournaments are held all over the country. These allow the participation of both foreign and Danish players on application to clubs.

For further information contact:
Dansk Tennis Forbund
Idrættens Hus, Brøndby Stadion 20,
DK-2605 Brøndby.
Tel: 43 26 26 60;
www.dtftennis.dk

Windsurfing

Given the country's close relationship with the sea, it is hardly surprising that windsurfing flourishes in Denmark. The long inlets and protected shores are excellent for beginners, while the open seas offer new challenges to experienced windsurfers. For further information contact: **Danish Sailboard Association**
Idrættens Hus, Brøndby Stadion 20,
DK-2605 Brøndby.
Tel: 43 26 21 82.

Sailing is hugely popular in Denmark, with its many sheltered inlets and extensive coastline

Food and drink

In major towns and cities, Danes eat out frequently, despite prices that seem high by the standards of other holiday destinations. Delicious open sandwiches, Denmark's favourite lunch snack, are far from cheap. Wine is very expensive and often mediocre. Finding a place to eat on a modest budget can be a challenge, but quality is almost always high. Most cities offer a wide choice of restaurants and cafés serving menus from around the world.

When the sun shines, café life spills on to Copenhagen's pavements

Vegetarian food

Vegetarians are not very well catered for in Denmark, and there are few specialist restaurants. In Copenhagen, serious veggies could do worse than to head for the alternative-culture enclave of Christiania, where the hippie ethos ensures the presence of a handful of purist vegetarian places.

Prices

In the restaurant listings below, the star ratings indicate the average cost per person for a meal, not including alcohol.

★   less than 200Dkr
★★   200–275Dkr
★★★   275–400Dkr
★★★★   more than 400Dkr

Prices are inclusive of cover charge, service charge and 25 per cent purchase tax (known as MOMS). Tipping is not standard, but 'rounding up' is common practice. The average cost of a bottle of wine in a restaurant is around 170–250Dkr.

Where to eat
COPENHAGEN
Bøf & Ost ★★★
Very popular French restaurant, next door to Peder Oxe's Vinkælder (*see* Cafés *opposite*).
Gråbødretorv 13.
Tel: 33 11 99 11.
Brede Spisehus ★★★
Charming traditional Danish restaurant located near the Frilandsmuseet.
IC Modewegs Vej.
Tel: 45 85 54 57.
Café Victor ★★
King of Copenhagen's café scene. Serves superb French food to well-heeled clientele.
Ny Østergade 8.
Tel: 33 13 36 13.
Cap Horn ★★
Excellent traditional Danish fare.
Nyhavn 21.
Tel: 33 12 85 04.
Egoisten ★★★
Recently refurbished, excellent French restaurant close to Hotel d'Angleterre.
Hovedvagtsgade 2.
Tel: 33 12 79 71.
Huset Med Det Grønne Træ ★
Back-to-basics traditional Danish *smørrebrød*.
Gammeltorv 20.
Tel: 33 12 87 86.
Kommandanten ★★★★
Michelin-starred Franco-Danish restaurant of exceptional standard.
Ny Adelgade 7.
Tel: 33 12 90 90.

Kong Hans Kælder ★★★★
A strikingly superb
restaurant in a 16th-
century cellar.
Vingårdstræde 6.
Tel: 33 11 68 68.

Konrad ★★★
One of the city's must-see
restaurants, serving
modern French-Danish
food. Stylish and sublime.
Pilestræde 12–14.
Tel: 33 93 29 29.

Krogs
Fiskerestaurant ★★★★
Copenhagen's most
exclusive seafood
restaurant.
Gammel Strand 38.
Tel: 33 15 89 15.

Passagens Spisehus ★★★
Traditional Nordic
ingredients with a
modern twist.
Vesterbrogade 42.
Tel: 33 22 47 57.

Pierre Andre ★★★★
Exceptional French
cuisine, very highly rated
by Danish newspapers.
Ny Østergade 9.
Tel: 33 16 17 19.

Restaurant Godt ★★★
Michelin-starred classic
French restaurant. Cosy
but stylish.
Gothersgade 38.
Tel: 33 15 21 22.

Restaurant Ida
Davidsen ★★
The queen of *smørrebrød*
presents the best of

Danish cuisine in this
cellar restaurant close to
Amalienborg.
Store Kongensgade 70.
Tel: 33 91 36 55.

Restaurant
Wiinblad ★★★★
The Hotel d'Angleterre's
excellent Franco-Danish
restaurant, overlooking
Kongens Nytorv.
Kongens Nytorv 34.
Tel: 33 12 00 95.

Søren K ★★
Minimalist modern
Danish harbourside
restaurant in the new
extension to the Royal
Library.
Søren Kierkegaard Plads 1.
Tel: 33 47 49 50.

TyvenKokkenHandsKone
og HendesElsker ★★★
Offers Copenhagen's
most imaginative menus
and is located in one of
its most charming streets.
Magstræde 16.
Tel: 33 16 12 92.

Zeleste ★★
Fusion courtyard
restaurant with outside
seating in summer.
Store Strandstræde 6.
Tel: 33 16 06 06.

Cafés
Amokka ★★
City's top café bar. Serves
excellent meals and cakes.
Dag Hammarskjolds Alle.
Tel: 33 25 35 35.

Bang og Jensen ★★
Hip and boho café in the
trendy Vesterbro quarter.
Istedgade 130.
Tel: 33 25 53 18.
Christianshavn Voldgade
50. Tel: 32 95 09 40.

Bastionen og Loven ★
Pretty outdoor café (with
some inside seating) on
the old ramparts of
Christianshavn.

Café a Porta ★★
Spectacular French-style
brasserie overlooking
Kongens Nytorv.
Kongens Nytorv 17.
Tel: 33 11 05 00.

Cafe Klimt ★
Arty café and bar with
excellent fusion kitchen.
Frederiksborggade 29.
Tel: 33 11 76 70.

Christianshavn
Bådudlejning Cafe ★
Floating café on a canal
in Christianshavn.
Overgaden Neden vandet
29. Tel: 32 96 53 53.

Dan Turell ★★
Glamorous Saturday-
night venue, also good
for Sunday brunch.
Sankt Regnegade 3–5.
Tel: 33 14 10 47.

Europa ★
Excellent café and
popular meeting spot,
located in central
Strøget.
Amagertorv 1.
Tel: 33 11 76 10.

Peder Oxe's Vinkælder ★★
Cosy cellar wine bar
in historic cobbled
square.
Gråbrødretorv 11.
Tel: 33 11 11 93.

Sebastopol ★★
Stylish brasserie; outdoor
seating in summer.
Guldbergsgade 2.
Tel: 35 36 30 02.

Wilder ★
Excellent place for a
down-to-earth open
sandwich, especially at
lunchtime.
Wildersgade 56.
Tel: 31 54 71 83.

Speciality cuisine
Ban-Gaw ★★
Excellent-value Thai food
down on Copenhagen's
sleazy sex street.
Istedgade 27.
Tel: 33 22 85 33.

Chico's Cantina ★★
A lively Mexican
restaurant with fun decor.
Borgergade 2.
Tel: 33 11 41 08.

Den Græske Taverna ★★
The city's best Greek
restaurant.
Rosenvængets Alle.
Tel: 35 26 74 43.

Era Ora ★★★★
The best Italian
restaurant in Denmark.
Very expensive.
Vandet 33B.
Tel: 32 54 06 93.

Flyvefisken ★★
Imaginative Thai food in
the groovy Pisserenden
area.
Larsbkornstræde 18.
Tel: 33 14 95 15.

Hercegovina ★★
Unusual restaurant
serving Balkan dishes.
Bernstorffsgade 3.
Tel: 33 15 63 63.

Illum ★★
Rooftop wok food and
pizzas in one of the top
department stores.
Østergade 52.
Tel: 33 18 28 00.

Pasta Basta ★★
Excellent Italian
restaurant; opens late.
Valkendorfsgade 22.
Tel: 33 11 21 31.

Riz Raz ★
Excellent value and
quality southern
European food.
Kannikestræde 19.
Tel: 33 32 33 45.

Spiseloppen ★★
Christiania's crazy fusion
restaurant, serving superb
quality and a unique
atmosphere.
*2nd floor of Loppen
Building, Bådmandsstræde
43, Christiania.*
Tel: 32 57 95 58.

Sushi Time ★★
Best-value sushi in town
– authentic too.
Grønnegade 28.
Tel: 33 11 88 99.

Taj Indian Restaurant ★
Spectacular decor and an
extensive menu of
authentic Indian food.
Jernbanegade 3–5.
Tel: 33 13 10 10.

AALBORG
Duus Vinkjælder ★★
Actually a wine bar in the
atmospheric vaults of
Jens Bang's house which
also serves meals and has
tables outside in summer.
Østeragade 9.
Tel: 98 12 50 56.

Hereford Beefstow ★★★
Best place in town for a
hearty steak.
Ved Stranden 7.
Tel: 98 12 75 22.

Kompasset ★★
Pub serving meals in the
maritime area.
Bådehavnsvej 11.
Tel: 98 13 75 00.

Mortens Kro ★★★
Probably the best in
Aalborg. Franco-Danish
cuisine.
Molleå 4–6.
Tel: 98 12 48 60.

Papegøjehaven ★★
Good value lunch buffets.
Europa Plads 2.
Tel: 98 12 54 99.

Prinses Juliana ★★★
Danish food aboard the
Prinses Juliana, moored at
Limfjord bridge.
Limfjord.
Tel: 98 11 55 66.

Provence ★★
French-Danish restaurant with budget lunches and a fuller range of dishes in the evenings. Good seafood.
Ved Stranden.
Tel: 98 13 51 33.

Rosdahls ★★
Back-to-basics French-Danish cooking using the best raw ingredients.
Strandvejen 6.
Tel: 98 12 05 80.

Stygge Krumpen ★★★
Seafood a speciality.
Vesterå 1. Tel: 98 16 87 87.

Speciality cuisine
China ★★
Chinese, plus a choice of international dishes.
10 Borgergade.
Tel: 98 13 74 80.

Layalina ★★★
Arabic restaurant.
Ved Stranden 7–9.
Tel: 98 11 60 56.

Merhaba ★★
Turkish restaurant with a good choice of dishes.
Østeragade 18C.
Tel: 98 12 14 09.

Mongolian Barbecue ★★
Classic Mongolian.
Jernbanegade 2.
Tel: 98 13 49 99.

Peking House ★
Excellent Chinese restaurant.
Vingaardsgade 5.
Tel: 98 13 19 11.

This restaurant offers panoramic views

Atypical day's eating in Denmark is rather like a thick sandwich – a hearty breakfast and dinner, with just a sliver of lunch wedged in between. The emphasis is on fresh ingredients and simple preparation, without much recourse to the exotic. There's almost no regional variation across the country.

First, the breakfast (*morgenmad*). In hotels or inns, a typical spread will include cereal, yoghurt, cheese (usually eaten with jam!), boiled eggs, pickled herring, cold meats, liver pâté, a huge selection of bread (led by thick hunks of white *franskbrød* and slender slices of dark rye *rugbrød*) and, of course, Danish pastries – called *wienerbrød* in Denmark. In fact, just about anything is served for breakfast except bacon, most of which is exported.

For lunch (*frokost*, which confusingly means breakfast in other Scandinavian languages) the *smørrebrød* open sandwich reigns supreme. A thin layer of bread is spread with a choice of toppings such as egg, cheese, salami, smoked salmon or pickled herring – either one of these, or a kaleidoscope of flavours on a single plate. *Smørrebrød* is served in a variety of sizes, as reflected in the prices, and is usually accompanied by a salad of fresh, raw vegetables.

Although sometimes served at lunchtime, hot dishes are generally reserved for dinner (confusingly known as *middag*). Fresh fish, simply prepared, can be outstanding; sole (*søtunge*), flounder (*hellefisk*) and halibut (*helleflynder*) from the North Sea or the Baltic can be superb steamed or lightly

fried in butter and served with vegetables and excellent Danish potatoes.

By far the most common meat dish is *frikadeller*, a meatball, usually of pork mixed with flour, egg, chopped onions and herbs, served with potatoes and thick gravy. It's a great filler and good value in restaurants. Pork can be excellent;

roasted loin (*helstegt svinekam*) is worth looking out for.

Meals tend to finish with fresh fruit or cheese rather than sweets. Even so, you should look out for *rødgrød med fløde* (redcurrant jelly with cream) whose notoriety owes much to the fact that foreigners find it the least pronounceable phrase in the entire Danish language.

Above: in Denmark, cheese is eaten at breakfast and also plays an important part in the famous open sandwich with its myriad toppings
Left: fresh fish is readily available everywhere, and (facing page) there is always something for the sweet-toothed shopper

BORNHOLM

Christianshøjkroen ★★★
Serves fish, game and other Bornholm delicacies out in the atmospheric Almingen forest.
Segenvej 48, Årkirkeby.
Tel: 56 97 40 13.

Di 5 Stauerna ★★★
A popular, top-quality hotel restaurant, open through the year.
Hotel Fredensborg.
Tel: 56 95 44 44.

Fyrtøjet ★★
Hans Christian Andersen 'fairytale' buffets (eat all you want).
Sankt Torvegade 22, Rønne.
Tel: 56 95 30 12.

ESBJERG

Bone's ★
Authentic American rib and beef restaurant.
Skolegade 17.
Tel: 75 13 61 18.

Dronning Louise ★★
Lively Danish restaurant and bar located in swinging Torvet. With live music Wednesday to Saturday.
Torvet 19.
Tel: 75 13 13 44.

Sand's Restaurant ★★★
Elegant and established Danish restaurant. Specialises in seafood.
Skolegade 60.
Tel: 75 12 02 07.

ODENSE

Brandts ★
Café and restaurant serving good-value lunchtime snacks.
Brandts Passage 35.
Tel: 66 14 00 49.

Restaurant Klitgaard ★★★
One of Odense's finest – French food based on the finest Danish ingredients.
Gravene 4.
Tel: 66 13 14 55.

Restaurant Kvægtorvet ★★★
Exceptional quality French-Danish restaurant, located in the old cattle market.
Rugårdsvej 25.
Tel: 65 91 50 01.

Restaurant Marie-Louise ★★★
Award-winning French restaurant.
Lottrups Gaard, Vestergade 70–72.
Tel: 66 19 19 95.

Restaurant Under Lindetræet ★★★
Superb modern food in a 19th-century setting.
Ramsherred 2.
Tel: 66 12 92 86.

ÅRHUS

Bone's ★
Classic American specialities.
Skolegade 33–35.
Tel: 86 13 27 55.

Bryggeriet Sct Clemens ★★
Pub with in-house brewery and meaty menu.
Kannikegade 10–12.
Tel: 86 13 80 00.

Café/Brasserie Le Coq ★★
Authentic French brasserie in the heart of Århus.
Graven 16.
Tel: 86 19 50 74.

L'Estragon ★★★
Cosy and exclusive French restaurant – mostly organic.
Klostergade 6.
Tel: 86 12 40 66.

Globen Flakket ★★
Brasserie-type restaurant over two floors. Good wine list.
Åboulevarden 18.
Tel: 87 31 03 33.

Malling Kro ★★★
Historic setting for superb Danish staples.
Stationspladsen 2, Malling.
Tel: 86 93 10 25.

Navigator ★★
On the harbour, serving superior seafood.
Marselisborg Havnevej 46d. Tel: 86 20 20 58.

Pinden ★★★
Excellent Danish cuisine.
Skolegade 29.
Tel: 86 12 11 02.

Restaurant Rene ★★★
Superb 1930s-style French restaurant, with one of Denmark's

largest wine cellars.
Hotel Ritz, Banegårds-pladsen 12.
Tel: 86 12 12 11.
Teater Bodega ★★
Traditional Danish restaurant close to Århus theatre.
Skolegade 7.
Tel: 86 12 19 17.
XO Bar and Restaurant ★★
Unusual and inventive restaurant and bar.
Sct. Clemens Torv 17.
Tel: 86 12 01 03.

Speciality cuisine
A/C ★★
Cool restaurant and bar with sushi and *yakatori.*

Klostertorv 5.
Tel: 86 12 95 67.
Athena ★
First-floor Greek restaurant with great views of the town's main square.
Store Torv, Borgporten 1.
Tel: 86 13 29 15.
Brazil ★★
Authentic gaucho food.
Scandic Hotel Plaza Århus, Banegårdspladsen.
Tel: 87 32 01 00.
Chinatown ★★
Authentic Chinese restaurant situated opposite the main bus station.
Fredensgade 46.
Tel: 86 19 62 64.
Hong Kong ★★
Hong Kong and

Cantonese specialities. Good value.
Europaplads 6.
Tel: 86 12 32 15.
Italia ★★
Pizzas cooked in a wood-fired oven. Steaks grilled at the table.
Åboulevarden 9.
Tel: 86 19 80 22.
Martino ★★
Large Italian restaurant in one of the city's most beautiful streets.
Marselisborg Havnevej 46b. Tel: 86 18 18 69.
Thai Mekong Restaurant ★★
Unusual Thai food, at the edge of the old town.
Vesterbrogade 36.
Tel: 86 13 16 37.

Odense has a broad sweep of bars and cafés in which to while away time

Drink

Moralists who find comfort in the restrictive attitudes that prevail towards drink in other Nordic countries may be disappointed in Denmark. The anti-drink lobby simply does not exist in any comparable fashion.

Although taxes on alcohol are high, and drinks in bars and restaurants can be seriously expensive, the Danes nevertheless drink with zest. Wines, beers and spirits can be purchased in grocery stores during normal shopping hours at comparatively low prices, and a huge selection of bars can be found open at any time.

For Danes, beer reigns supreme. The roots of this drink are deeply implanted in Danish culture; breweries are known to have existed in the 15th century and there is evidence that fermented drinks, flavoured with hops, were being made at least 200 years earlier. Today, Carlsberg and Tuborg, the country's two most popular brands, are both international names (though Tuborg is now owned by Carlsberg).

The Danes are also keen on their liqueurs, often served as chasers and knocked back with a glass of beer. Sweet brands are rarely drunk; *akvavit*, distilled from potatoes or grain, is preferred and is always served chilled. The drink comes in a variety of different forms, flavoured with caraway seeds, myrtle or dill and varying from colourless to pale gold. Aalborg is the main production centre. Gammel Dansk,

a Danish bitter with an endless list of ingredients, has the reputation for being a good hangover remedy. Whatever the truth of this, uninitiated palates generally find its taste hard to cope with.

Wine drinking and tasting also have a strong following in Denmark, and wine merchants and restaurateurs offer a wide selection of European and New World wines.

Carlsberg Pilsner

HUMBLE HOTEL Restaurant

'I drink therefore I am.' Tipping back a few beers is part of Danish philosophy

Hotels and accommodation

Hotels in Denmark range from sumptuous, historic five-star hotels such as Copenhagen's renowned Hotel d'Angleterre to luxurious business hotels such as those of the Radisson SAS group, represented in all Denmark's main cities (and throughout Scandinavia). Comfortable and affordable no-frills hotels such as those of the Cab-Inn group, with properties in Copenhagen, Århus, Aalborg and Esbjerg, are a good city alternative for those on a budget. In smaller towns and villages, in the country and at seaside resorts, there are affordable inns, farmhouses and holiday parks, campsites, and youth and family hostels.

Luxury hotels are well represented

In Copenhagen
As a rough guide, prices in the capital tend to be 30–40 per cent more

A contemporary hotel bedroom

expensive than elsewhere. Expect to pay up to 3,000Dkr per night for a double room in a 5-star hotel, including breakfast, tax and service charges. At the other end of the scale, it is possible to find a simple, clean, comfortable room in a 2-star, or equivalent, for 600–800Dkr.

Outside Copenhagen
Prices are lower and a full range of hotels is available in the main cities, plus various other types of accommodation, as listed below.

Camping
There are over 500 campsites in Denmark, classified by star ratings from one to five. One-star sites are rudimentary and provide just a drinking-water supply and basic washing and toilet facilities, while at the other end of the scale, 5-star sites come with pools, sports

halls, shops and cafés. At many sites it is also possible to rent caravans or cabins, where all you need bring is bed linen and towels. More details from: Campingrådet (*Hesseløgade 16, DK-2100, Copenhagen. Tel: 39 27 88 44; www.campingraadet.dk*).

Home exchange

Home exchange involves the home-swapping of two families for a given holiday period. The scheme welcomes overseas participants for whom the idea of free accommodation with direct access to real Danish culture (that is, a Danish home) is a major attraction.

Homes are usually fully equipped for youngsters.

For more information contact: **Dansk Boligbytte** (*Bernstorffsvej 71a, Box 53, DK-2900 Hellerup, tel: 39 61 04 05; www.bbdk.dk*).

Holiday centres

These self-contained resorts are found all over Denmark, though most of them are

Comprehensive listings of accommodation can be found on the Danish Tourist Board website (*www.visitdenmark.com*), and local tourist boards can help with booking and seasonal discounts.

Jutland has some charming, informal hotels

A youth hostel on Jutland – the standard of Danish hostels is a cut above most others

near the beach. Typically, they comprise apartments sleeping two to eight people. There is a restaurant and/or cafeteria, although kitchen facilities are available for those who want to do their own cooking. **Dansk Folkeferie** operates 11 holiday centres around the country. Contact them at: *Gammel Kongevej 33, DK-1610 Copenhagen; tel: 33 25 33 88; www.dansk-folkeferie.dk*

Contact the Danish Tourist Board for details of other companies.

Self-catering

Many Danish families own summer cottages, usually by a beach, which they rent out when not in use through local booking agents and tourist offices. They are well furnished and some have luxurious features such as indoor swimming pools, saunas and whirlpools. You need to bring your own towels and bed linen. An average cottage, sleeping six, costs upwards of 7,000Dkr per week in summer.

Youth and family hostels

Youth hostels are known as Danhostels in Denmark and offer a considerably higher degree of comfort than most of their counterparts elsewhere in Europe. Many have rooms with two or four beds, plus an en-suite bathroom. They provide an excellent means to explore Denmark on a budget, especially families (hence the renaming of what were formerly called simply 'Youth Hostels'). A valid membership card issued by your home country's Youth Hostel Association is recommended, or you can buy one from a Danish hostel. Overnight stays cost 100Dkr per person in dormitory accommodation and 150–500Dkr in private rooms. Breakfast and dinner are extra.

For more information, contact: **Danhostel Danmarks Vandrerhjem**, Central Booking, *Vesterbrogade 39, DK-1620 Copenhagen; tel: 33 31 36 12; www.danhostel.dk*

Seaside campers at Tranum, Jutland. Sites come with varying facilities

On business

The Danes are scrupulously punctual in their business dealings. If they foresee the likelihood of being so much as five minutes late for an appointment, they will probably telephone apologetically. Underlying this is what some people regard as an almost obsessional dependence on the telephone: business associates may speak to each other several times a day, where in other countries a single, longer call would be the more usual approach.

SAS is the main business airline to Denmark

Dress
In matters of dress, Danes are less formal than people in many parts of Europe. Blazers or sports jackets, worn with a tie, can substitute for business suits.

Business hours
Normal office hours: 8/9am–4/5pm. Banking hours: 9.30am–4pm, Monday to Friday, and till 6pm on Thursday.

Conferences and exhibitions
COPENHAGEN
Bella Center *Tel: 32 52 88 11*; *www.bellacenter.dk*
Radisson SAS Falconer Hotel & Congress Center
Tel: 0800 33 33 33 33.

ÅRHUS
Århus Congress Center
Tel: 86 13 88 44.

Economic Indicators 2006
Money
Inflation: 1.8 per cent.
GDP (US$): 263.4 billion.
GDP growth rate: 2.7 per cent.

Employment
Unemployment percentage: 10.7.
For all other relevant and up-to-date statistical information, business visitors should contact the relevant Danish Embassy; visit the website of the Royal Danish Ministry of Foreign Affairs at *www.um.dk*, from which full statistical reports of the Danish economy may be ordered or downloaded (most recent available: 2003/04); or visit the website of Danmarks Statistik *www.dts.dk*

Stock exchange
The KFX Index is a key index made up of the 20 most actively traded shares on the Copenhagen stock exchange. Share and bond information can be found on Danmarks Radio teletext pages 554–63.

Secretarial services, interpreters and translators
The largest business hotel group in Denmark and Scandinavia, Radisson SAS Hotels, offers full in-house translation and secretarial services at all its city hotels, as do most other major business hotels in Denmark. Messenger

services, photocopying, mobile
telephone rental and computer rental
are also most easily arranged through
your business hotel.

COPENHAGEN
Copenhagen City Business Center
Grabrodretorv 1. Tel: 33 33 88 33.
Regus Business Center *Larsbjornstrade 3.
Tel: 33 32 25 25.*
Compactas *Vesterbrogade 32, 1620
Copenhagen V. Tel: 33 25 65 10.*
Inter-set *Vesterbrogade 32, 1620
Copenhagen V. Tel: 33 25 04 11.*

ÅRHUS
Karin Lange *Tel: 86 13 81 00.*

Messenger service
De Gronne Bud *Blagardsgade 22.
Tel: 31 39 31 39.*
Budstikken *Niels Ebbesensvej 17, 1911
Frederiksberg C. Tel: 31 24 62 00.*

Photocopying
Vesterkopi *Vesterbrogade 69.
Tel: 33 27 88 33.*
Nyhavns Kopi Center
*Holbergsgade 14. Tel: 33
93 05 33.*
Prontaprint *Gl. Kongevej
82, 1850 Frederiksberg C.
Tel: 31 22 23 36.*

Mobile telephone rental
Telecom Center *Kastrup
Airport (Transit Hall). Tel:
32 52 00 22.*
Talkline *Gl. Kongevej 9,
1600 Copenhagen K. Tel:
31 31 18 41.*

Computer rental
Dataudlejning *Vangedevej 233, 2860
Soborg. Tel: 31 56 41 06.*
AV-DUS *A. Nielsens Boulavarden
124–126. Tel: 31 49 52 01; fax: 31 49 57 43.*

Useful addresses
For the addresses of relevant government
ministries and agencies, industrial and
business organisations, trade unions and
employers' associations, and investment
funds, contact the Danish Embassy in
your home country or the Danish
Chamber of Commerce.

**Danish Federation of Employers for
Trade, Transport and Services (HTSA)**
*Sundrogskaj 20, 2100 Copenhagen.
Tel: 70 13 12 00; www.htsa.dk*
**Det Danske Handeslkammer Borsen
(Danish Chamber of Commerce)**
*Copenhagen. Tel: 70 13 12 00;
www.hts.dk*
Danish-UK Chamber of Commerce
*55 Sloane Street, London SW1X 9SR.
Tel: 020 7823 1200; www.ducc.co.uk*

The solid block of buildings that houses the Danish National Bank

Practical guide

Arriving
Entry formalities
Citizens of European Union (EU) countries that are part of the Schengen agreement and of other Scandinavian countries do not officially require passports but must have an identity card or another accepted form of identification carrying a photograph of the holder. Citizens of all other countries including the UK require a full passport. It is recommended that the passport should have a minimum of six months' validity upon entering the country.

Visas
No visas are required by EU citizens or those of Australia, Canada, New Zealand and the USA for stays of up to 90 days. Citizens of the Republic of South Africa require a visa.

By air
Scandinavian Airlines (*tel: 0870 607 27 727; www.flysas.com*) has the largest network of flights to Denmark from the UK, with services to Copenhagen from London Heathrow, London City, Birmingham, Manchester, Newcastle and Aberdeen. SAS also flies from Ireland, mainland Europe, the Asia-Pacific region, North America and Africa, with direct flights to Copenhagen and other Danish cities from almost all European capital cities and major regional airports. SAS also has an extensive network of routes from Denmark to the rest of Scandinavia and, through its membership of the Star

Alliance airline network, the rest of the world.

Copenhagen's Kastrup International Airport is one of the most modern in Europe and is only 8km (5 miles) and 20 minutes from the city centre by fast, clean and reliable trains. It is also easily accessible from Malmö in Sweden via the Øresund road-rail bridge.

Other airlines serving Denmark from the UK include BMI (*tel: 0870 6070 555; www.flybmi.com*) to Copenhagen from Glasgow and Edinburgh, and Esbjerg from Aberdeen; British Airways (*tel: 0870 850 9850; www.ba.com*) to Copenhagen from Heathrow, Birmingham and Manchester, and Billund from Manchester; easyJet (*tel: 0871 7500 100; www.easyjet.com*) to Copenhagen from Stansted, Bristol and Newcastle; Ryanair (*tel: 08712 460 000; www.ryanair.com*) to Århus and Esbjerg from Stansted; and Sterling (*tel: 020 7333 0066; www.sterling.dk*) to Copenhagen from London Gatwick and Edinburgh, and to Aalborg from Gatwick.

By sea
DFDS Seaways (*tel: 08702 520 524; www.dfds.co.uk*) operates passenger and car ferries and mini-cruises from Harwich to Esbjerg. For those wishing to combine a trip to Denmark with a visit to its Scandinavian neighbours, DFDS also sails from Newcastle to Kristiansand in Norway and Gothenburg in Sweden, and from Copenhagen to Helsingborg in Sweden. Crossings take around 20 hours on fast,

modern cruise-ferries with an array of on-board activities and entertainment and a choice of comfortable and luxurious cabin accommodation.

By rail

There are direct train services to Denmark from Germany and Sweden, and boat trains from Norway and the UK. Inter-Rail tickets are valid in Denmark.

The *Thomas Cook European Rail Timetable* is published monthly and gives up-to-date details of most rail services and many shipping services throughout Europe; this will help plan a rail journey to, from and around Denmark. In the UK it is available to buy from *www.thomascookpublishing. com*, some railway stations, any branch of Thomas Cook or by calling *01733 416477*. In the USA, contact SF Travel Publications, *tel: 1 800 322 3834; e-mail: sales@travelbookstore.com; www.travelbookstore.com*

By road

There is a motorway border crossing with Germany near Frøslev and seven other road frontiers in south Jutland. For Zealand, drivers from Germany can take a ferry from Puttgarden via Lolland Island, or Warnemünde via Falster Island. A bridge, scheduled to open here in 2012, will link Germany with Denmark by road.

Camping

Denmark has hundreds of well-equipped campsites beside the sea, in the countryside and near major cities. Some offer tented or mobile home accommodation for those without their own tent. For information and bookings, contact the Dansk Camping Union, *Korsdalsvej 134, 2605 Brøndby. Tel: 33 21 06 00; www.dcu.dk* or *DK-Camp (the national association of private campsites), Industrivej 5D, 7120 Velje. Tel: 75 71 29 62; www.dk-camp.dk. See pp172–3.*

Tourists enjoying the sea at Grenen

Children

Facilities for children are among the best in the world (*see pp156–7*). Many museums and other tourist attractions offer reduced or free admission to children.

Climate

Denmark has a relatively mild maritime climate, generally free of extremes. Summers are usually warm and sunny, although rain is a possibility at any time of year. Winters can be cold, with the probability of snow between late December and February, though it is seldom severe. May and June can be cold and wet. July and August are the peak tourist months and temperatures can reach highs of 30°C (86°F).

Conversion tables

See opposite.
Clothes and shoe sizes follow the standard sizes for the Rest of Europe.

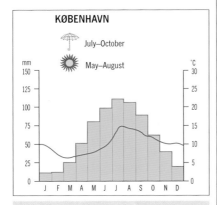

KØBENHAVN

July–October

May–August

Weather Conversion Chart
25.4mm = 1 inch
°F = 1.8 x °C + 32

Crime

Denmark is generally a very safe country and crime is rarely a problem for tourists. Nevertheless, nobody should be lulled into a false sense of security; cars should always be left locked, and luggage and other valuables removed from sight.

As in most European cities, drug-related crime is on the increase in Copenhagen and care should be taken at night, particularly around the railway station and in the vicinity of Christiania. If you are robbed, report the incident to the police immediately and ask for a copy of the statement; this will be needed for any insurance claim.

Customs regulations

Visitors to Denmark arriving from another European Union (EU) member country need not complete customs formalities. Non-EU visitors should check notices on points of entry for quantities of tobacco, wine, spirits, beer, foodstuffs and other goods for which there are entry restrictions.

Driving

Denmark has an excellent network of uncluttered roads which amply support the relatively sparse traffic. One of the best means of touring Denmark with time on your hands is to follow the **Marguerit-rute** (Marguerite Route) – over 3,400km (2,113 miles) of minor roads and winding lanes reaching every forgotten corner of the country. Distinctive brown, white and yellow signs point the way from just about everywhere in Denmark.

Accidents and breakdowns

All accidents must be reported to the Dansk Forening for International Motorkøretøjsforsikring, *Amaliegade 10, DK-1256 Copenhagen* (*tel: 33 43 55 00; www.forsikringsoplysningen.dk*). If another vehicle is involved, insurance details should be swapped with the other driver. Notify your insurer as soon as possible. In case of serious accident, phone *112* (toll free) for the emergency services as soon as possible. If you break down, call one of the two national organisations, Falck or Dansk Autohjalp, which operate a 24-hour service from over 100 centres, for which you will be charged. If necessary, they will tow you to a garage. On motorways, both organisations can be called from the emergency telephones. If you need vehicle repair and can get your own car to a garage, find one listed under *Automobil reparation* in the *Yellow Pages* phone book.

Alcohol

Drink-driving offences are punished by strict penalties.

Documents

If you bring your own car into Denmark from abroad, you will need a full (not provisional) UK or EU driving licence and the car's registration documents. A green card is also highly recommended, though not required by law. A nationality badge or sticker must be displayed on the rear of the vehicle.

Fuel

The majority of fuel stations in Denmark are self-service; some are unattended, with automatic pumps

Conversion Table

FROM	TO	MULTIPLY BY
Inches	Centimetres	2.54
Feet	Metres	0.3048
Yards	Metres	0.9144
Miles	Kilometres	1.6090
Acres	Hectares	0.4047
Gallons	Litres	4.5460
Ounces	Grams	28.35
Pounds	Grams	453.6
Pounds	Kilograms	0.4536
Tons	Tonnes	1.0160

To convert back, for example from centimetres to inches, divide by the number in the third column.

Men's Suits

UK		36	38	40	42	44	46	48
Rest of Europe	46	48	50	52	54	56	58
USA		36	38	40	42	44	46	48

Dress Sizes

UK		8	10	12	14	16	18
France		36	38	40	42	44	46
Italy		38	40	42	44	46	48
Rest of Europe		34	36	38	40	42	44
USA		6	8	10	12	14	16

Men's Shirts

UK	14	14.5	15	15.5	16	16.5	17
Rest of Europe	36	37	38	39/40	41	42	43
USA	14	14.5	15	15.5	16	16.5	17

Men's Shoes

UK		7	7.5	8.5		9.5	10.5	11
Rest of Europe	41	42	43	44	45	46
USA		8	8.5	9.5	10.5	11.5	12

Women's Shoes

UK		4.5	5	5.5	6	6.5	7
Rest of Europe	38	38	39	39	40	41
USA		6	6.5	7	7.5	8	8.5

accepting 200, 100 and 50Dkr notes as payment. Three unleaded grades are available (*blyfri* – available in 98, 95 and 92 octanes). Leaded petrol is no longer commonly available. Diesel is also sold at all fuel stations.

Laws

Drive on the right and overtake on the left. Unless otherwise indicated, give way to traffic on the right. At junctions and roundabouts give way to pedestrians crossing the road you are entering. Front seat belts must be worn, as well as back seat belts if fitted. Also pay attention to cyclists, who often use the far-right lane in cities, and have the right of way.

Unless otherwise stated, speed limits are 50km/h (30mph) in built-up areas, 80km/h (50mph) outside built-up areas and 110km/h (68mph) on motorways. For anyone towing a caravan or other trailer, the maximum speed limit is 70km/h (44mph). Built-up areas are signalled by town name signs which also have a silhouette of buildings. A similar sign with a diagonal red line through it signals the end of the built-up area limit.

Lights

As in other Scandinavian countries, it is compulsory to use dipped headlights whenever the car is being driven. This applies no matter how bright the sunlight. Drivers of right-hand drive vehicles must use beam deflectors; these are widely available in motoring shops and at Channel ports.

Motorcycling

Helmets must be worn at all times by riders and pillion passengers. As with other vehicles, dipped headlights should be used at all times.

Motoring organisations

The main Danish motoring organisation is the Forenede Danske Motorejere, *Firskovvej 32, PO Box 500, DK-2800 Lyngby (tel: 45 93 08 00; www.fdm.dk)*. The FDM offers legal and technical assistance to members of organisations affiliated to the AIT (Alliance Internationale de Tourisme), including Britain's Automobile Association (AA).

Parking

Danish cars are fitted with parking dials (called P-Skive), resembling a clock, displayed on the front windscreen or dashboard. If you are bringing your own car into the country, stop and buy one at any fuel station. In many towns parking is free for a finite period as indicated by signs such as *2 timer* (2 hours); set the dial to the nearest quarter of an hour to your arrival time, and be sure to move on before the indicated span of time has expired.

Other towns have pay-and-display car parks (*Parkeringsbillet påkrævet*). In these, stickers are purchased from a machine and displayed on the windscreen interior.

Rental

Large international companies and smaller local ones are widely advertised and easy to find, although charges are relatively high. It can be cheaper to book a car in advance from your home country.

By law, you must be over 20 years old to hire a car, but some companies insist on drivers being at least 23, and sometimes 25.

Electricity
The electric current is 220 volts AC (50Hz) and sockets are for continental two-point plugs. An adaptor will be needed for UK appliances fitted with a three-point plug, and a voltage transformer for appliances from the USA and Canada.

Embassies and consulates
Australia *26 Dampfærgevej, DK-2100 Copenhagen.*
Tel: 70 26 36 76.

Canada *1 Kristen Bernikowsgade, DK-1105 Copenhagen.*
Tel: 33 48 32 00.
Republic of Ireland *Østbanegade 21, DK-2100 Copenhagen.*
Tel: 35 42 32 33.
United Kingdom *36–40 Kastelsvej, DK-2100 Copenhagen.*
Tel: 35 44 52 00.
USA *24 Dag Hammerskjolds Allé, DK-2100 Copenhagen.*
Tel: 33 41 71 00.

Emergency telephone number
Accidents, Police, Fire or Ambulance
112 (toll free from public call boxes).

Busy Copenhagen is surprisingly pedestrian-friendly

Health

There are no mandatory vaccination requirements. It is recommended that travellers keep tetanus and polio immunisation up to date. As with every other part of the world, AIDS is present. Food and water are considered safe.

All EU countries have reciprocal arrangements for reclaiming the cost of medical services. UK and EU residents should obtain the European Health Insurance Card, which entitles the bearer to free or reduced cost, state-provided medical treatment in Denmark and anywhere in the European Economic Area. The EHIC is free and application forms are available at any post office, by phoning *0845 605 0707* or at *www.dh.gov.uk/travellers*. Claiming is often a long-drawn-out process and you are covered only for medical care, not for emergency repatriation, holiday cancellation and so on. You are strongly advised to take out a travel insurance policy to cover all eventualities.

Hitch-hiking

Hitching is not widely practised in Denmark and is seldom worth the effort. It is illegal on motorways.

Insurance

Travel insurance should be taken out before leaving to cover property loss and theft, as well as medical costs and accident cover. For drivers, third-party cover is the legal minimum but fully comprehensive cover is advisable.

Maps

Maps are available from tourist offices all over Denmark, generally free of

LANGUAGE

Danish is a Germanic language, close to Swedish and Norwegian, and many words are similar to German. But it is a difficult language to pronounce because some letters (d, g) are silent in the middle or at the end of words, h before a v becomes silent, and some specifically Scandinavian vowels (æ, ø, å), are awkward to say correctly. But the Danes are aware of this problem and most speak very good English. The following words should help you to get around and read menus (which are often also in English and German).

yes	ja
no	nej
please	vær så venlig
thank you	tak
hello (informal)	hej
goodbye	farvel
good morning	godmorgen
good afternoon	goddag
good evening	godaften
good night	godnat
entrance	indgang
no entry	ingen adgang
	(for pedestrians)
exit	udgang
no exit	ingen udgang
emergency exit	nødudgang
push/pull	skub/træk or
	tryk/træk
ladies	damer
gentlemen	herrer
toilets	toiletter
open	åben
close	lukket
no smoking	rygning forbudt
arrival	ankomst

departure	afgang	**pork**	flæsk, svine
timetable	køreplan	**chicken**	kylling
town plan	bykort	**boiled chicken**	høne/hønse
step down/up	trin ned /op	**white bread**	franskbrød
no standing	rejs Dem ikke op	**rye bread**	rugbrød
		French bread	flûte
Monday	mandag	**Danish pastry**	Wienerbrød
Tuesday	tirsdag	**butter**	smør
Wednesday	onsdag	**shellfish**	skaldyr
Thursday	torsdag	**herring**	sild
Friday	fredag	**trout**	ørred
Saturday	lørdag	**cod**	torsk
Sunday	søndag	**shrimps**	rejer
		vegetables	grøntsager
opening times	åbningstider	**onion**	løg
o'clock	klokken	**peas**	ærter
exhibition	udstilling	**potatoes**	kartofler
petrol	benzin	**red cabbage**	rødkål
car	bil	**carrot**	gulerod
do not touch	må ikke berøres	**cheese**	ost
railway	station banegård	**fruit salad**	frugtsalat
railway line	jernbane		
street	gade	**coffee/tea**	kaffe/te
ferry	færge	**house wine**	husets vin
no entry	(cars) ingen indkørsel	**red/white**	rød/hvid
Great Britain	Storbritannien	**apple juice**	æblemost
USA	De Forenede Stater	**orange juice**	appelsinjuice
		full cream milk	sødmælk
FOOD		**low fat milk**	letmælk
breakfast	morgenmad	**skimmed milk**	skummetmælk
lunch	frokost		
dinner	middagsmad	**NUMBERS**	
starters	forretter	**1**	en
soups	supper	**2**	to
main courses	hovedretter	**3**	tre
fish dishes	fiskeretter	**4**	fire
cold dishes	fra det kolde køkken	**5**	fem
hot dishes	fra det varme køkken	**6**	seks
baked	bagt	**7**	syv
roast	helstegt, steg	**8**	otte
steamed	dampet	**9**	ni
smoked	røget	**10**	ti

charge. Some can also be obtained from Danish Tourist Board Offices in your home country.

Media

The Copenhagen Post (*www.cphpost.dk*) is the capital's English-language newspaper. Various European newspapers are available in Copenhagen and other cities from the afternoon of the day of publication.

English-language satellite television stations are received in most good hotels.

Radio Denmark broadcasts news in English from Monday to Friday at 8.30am on Programme 1 (94.5 MHz).

Money matters

Denmark, though part of the EU, has not adopted the euro. The Danish kroner (Dkr), divided into 100 øre, remains as the accepted currency. Banknotes are issued in 1,000, 500, 200, 100 and 50 kroner denominations, and coins in 20, 10, 5 and 1 kroner, plus 50 and 25 øre.

Currency exchange

Outside bank opening hours (*see opposite*), money can be exchanged in most good hotels.

Money can also be changed out of hours at Copenhagen's railway station, at the Magasin and Salling department stores in Århus and at the Aalborg tourist office.

Credit cards and cheques

International credit and charge cards are widely accepted throughout Denmark. Traveller's cheques free you from the hazards of carrying large sums of cash, and in the event of loss or theft can be quickly refunded. Hotels and restaurants will generally accept traveller's cheques; good-quality shops may do the same.

Cash machines

Automatic cash dispensers (called *kontanten*), to be found in Copenhagen and other major cities, can be used to draw Danish currency using all credit, debit and charge cards bearing the Maestro or Cirrus symbols.

Taxes

Many good-quality shops operate a tax refund system (*see p142*).

National holidays

1 January New Year's Day
April/May, variable Maundy Thursday, Good Friday, Easter Sunday, Easter
  Monday
**April/May, fourth Friday after Good
  Friday** Common Prayer Day
May/June, 40th day after Easter
  Ascension Day
May/June, 50th day after Easter
  Whit Monday
5 June Constitution Day
24 December Christmas Eve
25 December Christmas Day
26 December Boxing Day
31 December New Year's Eve

Opening hours
Shops

Shopping hours vary between towns. In Copenhagen, typical opening times are 10am–5.30pm Monday to Friday and 10am–1pm on Saturday. On the Strøget in July and August, however, many shops are open until late, seven days a week.

In most other cities and towns, shops open from 9 or 10am to 5.30pm Monday to Thursday, staying open later on Fridays, and from 9am to 1pm on Saturdays. On the first and last Saturday of each month many shops also open from 4 to 5pm.

Banks
Banking hours are 10am to 4pm Monday to Friday. Unibank stays open till 5pm, and all banks are open till 6pm on Thursday.

Pharmacies
Most towns have a centrally located *apotek* (pharmacy), open during normal shopping hours, although larger cities will have one open 24 hours. These are generally listed in tourist leaflets. It is important that travellers bring a supply of prescribed medicines to cover their entire stay in Denmark, as some pharmacists may only dispense drugs prescribed by Scandinavian doctors.

Places of worship
Although religious observance is minimal in Denmark, Sunday services are held in churches throughout the country. In Copenhagen, church services are conducted in English for the following Christian denominations: International Baptist, First Church of Christ Scientist, Church of England, Methodist, International Pentecostal and Roman Catholic. Times are published in *Copenhagen This Week*, available from the tourist office free of charge. There are nearly 40 mosques (official and private) in Copenhagen, and one synagogue (*tel: 39 29 95 20*).

Senior citizens
Recipients of state pensions in their home countries are entitled to reductions on Danish railways on presentation of their passport and a senior citizen travel card. All UK travellers over 60 who hold a Senior Railcard are eligible for a 30 per cent discount on Danish railways.

Sustainable tourism
Thomas Cook is a strong advocate of ethical and fairly traded tourism and believes that the travel experience should be as good for the places visited as it is for the people who visit them. That's why we firmly support The Travel Foundation, a charity that develops solutions to help improve and protect holiday destinations, their environment, traditions and culture. To find out what you can do to make a positive difference to the places you travel to and the people who live there, please visit *www.thetravelfoundation.org.uk*

Telephones
Denmark has an efficient system for internal and international calls. It is much cheaper to use a public payphone than to call from your hotel room. Public phones accept coins, credit cards or prepaid phonecards, available from news kiosks, selected shops and post offices. Most phones have instructions in English and operators are usually fluent in English. Mobile phone coverage is excellent nationwide.

International codes
Denmark's country code is *00 45*.

To dial abroad from Denmark, simply dial the country code, preceded by *00*:

Australia *61*
Canada or the **USA** *1*
New Zealand *64*
Republic of Ireland *353*
Republic of South Africa *27*
United Kingdom *44*
Then dial the area code (omitting any initial zero), followed by the number.

Time
Denmark is on GMT plus 1 hour (that is, 1 hour ahead of Britain and Ireland, 6 hours ahead of US Eastern Standard Time and 11 hours behind Sydney).

Tipping
Tipping is not the norm in Denmark. Service is already included in restaurant bills and taxi fares.

Toilets
Public toilets (*toiletter*) are among the cleanest in Europe and generally free of charge. There are separate toilets for men and women (*Herrer/Damer*) as indicated by the standard international pictographs.

Tourist offices
Denmark has an excellent network of tourist information offices (*Turistinformationen*). Most towns have a centrally located and well signposted office, always with English-speaking staff. As well as providing information they will book local accommodation for no charge. You will find the address and telephone numbers of tourist offices in the relevant gazetteer section of this guide.

Even dogs have their own clean toilet disposals

Equally efficient and helpful are the Visit Denmark offices abroad:
UK (including Ireland) Visit Denmark, *55 Sloane Street, London SW1X 9SY. Tel: (020) 7259 5959.*
USA Visit Denmark, *655 Third Avenue, New York, NY 10017. Tel: (212) 885 97 00.*

Travellers with disabilities
Denmark is generally better equipped than virtually any other country to deal with the needs of travellers with disabilities. Facilities are second to none, with most good hotels, airports, railway stations and trains, ferry terminals and ferries, museums and public toilets providing access for people with disabilities. The Danish Tourist Board publishes *Access in Denmark – A Travel Guide for the Disabled*, a free booklet listing facilities for travellers with disabilities throughout the country, including the distance between tourist attractions and their car parks. Also contact Danish Handicap Association, Hans Knudsens Plads 1A, DK-2100 Copenhagen (*tel: 39 29 35 55; www.dhf-net.dk*).

ACKNOWLEDGEMENTS
Thomas Cook Publishing wishes to thank the following photographers, libraries and associations for their assistance in the preparation of this book, to whom the copyright in the photographs belongs.

BANG & OLUFSEN 146; ROBIN GAULDIE 1, 7, 10, 33, 39, 40, 43, 44a, 46b, 83, 86b, 93b, 104, 111, 113, 144, 147, 150, 155, 157, 161, 162, 165, 176, 183; DFDS 134; CHILI FOTO & ARKIV 12, 91, 103, 121, 140, 145, 154, 159, 172a; DANISH TOURIST BOARD 15 (Ireneusz Cyranek); 16 (Nicolai Perjesi); 70, 94, 138 (Cees Van Roeden); 66, 67 (Jan Kofoed Winther); 80 (Mikkel Grabowski); 151 (Thomas Petri); 172b (Skt Petri); 51 (Niels Thyge); 143 and 173; HENRIK STENBERG 13, 14, 34; MARY EVANS PICTURE LIBRARY 11; MOESGARD MUSEUM, DENMARK 118; PETER HAUERBACH 177; PICTURES COLOUR LIBRARY 2, 3, 19, 20, 46a, 65, 95, 129a, 131, 132, 133, 148, 149; JIM STEINHART of www.PlanetWare.com 53, 55, 73; RUDY HEMMINGSEN 130; SWEDISH TRAVEL AND TOURISM COUNCIL 135 (Kjell Holmner/Goteborg & Co./imagebank.sweden.se); SILKEBORG MUSEUM, DENMARK 119; SPECTRUM COLOUR LIBRARY 4, 18b, 58, 78, 79b, 105, 114, 129b
The remaining pictures are held in the AA PHOTO LIBRARY and were taken by: JESPER WESTLEY JORGENSEN, with the exception of pages 30, 48, 76, 82, 86a, 88, 99 and 174, which were taken by DEREK FORSS.

Copy-editing: PENNY ISAAC

Index: MARIE LORIMER

Maps: PC GRAPHICS, SURREY, UK

Proof-reading: JAN McCANN for CAMBRIDGE PUBLISHING MANAGEMENT LTD

Send your thoughts to
books@thomascook.com

We're committed to providing the very best up-to-date information in our travel guides and constantly strive to make them as useful as they can be. You can help us to improve future editions by letting us have your feedback. If you've made a wonderful discovery on your travels that we don't already feature, if you'd like to inform us about recent changes to anything that we do include, or if you simply want to let us know your thoughts about this guidebook and how we can make it even better – we'd love to hear from you.

Send us ideas, discoveries and recommendations today and then look out for your valuable input in the next edition of this title. And, as an extra 'thank you' from Thomas Cook Publishing, you'll be automatically entered into our exciting monthly prize draw.

Emails to the above address, or letters to Travellers Project Editor, Thomas Cook Publishing, PO Box 227, Unit 18, Coningsby Road, Peterborough PE3 8SB, UK.

Please don't forget to let us know which title your feedback refers to!